AMONG THE DERVISHES

AMONG THE DERVISHES

by

O. M. Burke

*An account of travels in Asia and Africa, and
four years studying the Dervishes, Sufis
and Fakirs, by living among them.*

A Dutton  *Paperback*

NEW YORK
E. P. DUTTON & CO., INC.
1975

This paperback edition of

AMONG THE DERVISHES

First published 1975 by E. P. Dutton & Co., Inc.

Copyright © 1973 by Omar Michael Burke
All rights reserved. Printed in the U.S.A.

FIRST EDITION

10 9 8 7 6 5 4 3 2 1

Published simultaneously in Canada by Clarke, Irwin & Company Limited, Toronto and Vancouver
ISBN: 0-525-47386-6

1. Sufism

2   Burke, Omar Michael

3   Middle East — Description and travel

Contents

Preface

It was largely through a series of lucky chances that I made the contacts and carried out the journeys whose accounts were published in *Blackwood's Magazine*. Its Editor had given me my first chance to appear in print.

Through living in a Sufi monastery and visiting dervish communities in North Africa, I learned a certain amount at first hand about a philosophy whose adherents are numbered by the million, and are much more widespread than those of any other mystical system.

I returned to Europe determined to perfect my knowledge of this strange and interesting cult by studying the literature available in Western languages. To my absolute astonishment, I found that Sufism was generally treated as a matter of academic study, and a 'dead' one at that. True, literally hundreds of absorbing books, the fruit of many generations of research, had been published, notably in English; but there was no single scrap of evidence, internal or otherwise, that the majority of students of Sufism who had published their laborious work had ever associated with practising Sufis. Between the Western imitations of Sufi circles, pale imitations at that, and the other extreme of arid scholasticism there was almost nothing.

Even those few writers, mostly what are called by the academics 'popularisers' who had been in contact with dervishes were almost always already in the mental grip of some doctrine, through the filter of which they 'interpreted' Sufism. Of sociological or anthropological work there was virtually none. In the purely literary field, although almost every Sufi classic book had been translated, the interpretations were inaccurate or insufficient.

I therefore resolved to travel to as many Eastern lands as my resources would permit, to spend as much time as might be needed, to look for and record as much as possible about the people who believe that they are responsible for passing down a teaching destined to play a major part in the human story.

Not least of the interesting facts encountered was the emphasis upon values and traditions which are, although nominally Eastern, perceptibly identical with some of the most cherished principles upon which our own society rests.

This book is dedicated to those who, by suggesting that I might write it, gave me the encouragement which I would never otherwise have had.

Its only justification is that it contains as high a proportion as possible of entirely fresh and first-hand material.

Synopsis

with Fikri Bey, the ancient Sufi. Journey to the tomb of Jalaluddin Rumi. Remarks about Rumi. The story of the clipped
bird. The elephant in the darkened house. Decision to visit
India.

Chapter 9: *Damascus*

Feeling of this ancient city. Meeting with Khalid, son of Tarzi. His house, the people collected there. Descriptions of the Studious King, visiting the sick, healing capacities; how a man got a job unexpectedly. Is the Sufi teaching the 'inner lore of Islam'? Prescience attributed to the Shah; walking upon water; deceit in a business matter. Meeting with Samir Pasha. His opinions about the role of the Sufi chief.

Chapter 10: *The Murshid Speaks*

Meeting with the Shah; interest in juvenile delinquency. The reasons for writing a book may be other than they seem; the husk and the kernel of the Koran. Psychic powers and their meaning. People talk in proverbs without real meaning. How a Sufi fills a vacuum. Meaning of certain phrases.

Chapter 11: *Nasnas and Wiswas*

The problems of organisations; how a person imprisons himself with his ideas. The temporary value of system in thought. The Complete Man; the Remnant Cults; ritual as seen by the Sufi; natural laws and the Cults; the role of priesthood in ancient times; the exercise of conscious baraka; the use of hypnosis; the 'work' and how it is carried on. The Malayan phenomenon called *Latah*; subjective states called Wiswas and Nasnas. The impatience of students.

Chapter 12: *The Richest Man Alive*

Meeting with the Sheikh of Kuwait. Guest of Sheikh Abdallah el-Sabah; a straight talker; his account of the Sufi Foundation; how it operates; secret charity; his observations about Saint Nicholas. I leave for Cairo.

Chapter 13: *Suleiman Bey*

Suleiman Bey meets me in Cairo. Relics and Monasteries. The School of the Masters, which stands behind the Sufi Orders. The basic teaching of Bahauddin Naqshband of Bokhara. The books called Drops from the Fount of Life and The Book of Wisdom. The nature of the 'Foundation', entrusted with the dervish lore; connections with the Assassins. The secret leaders of the Moslems, hidden Imams.

11

Among the Dervishes

Chapter 14 : *The Secret of the Teacher*
The argument that the West lacks spirituality; this is not so. Baghdad and a meeting with the chief of the Sufis. Answering unspoken questions. The people who understand, and where they are; how they operate. The real teachers. Teaching to the Sufis is team-work; a strange concept to us. The Dervish reverence for Jesus. Assumptions made in trying to find a spiritual teaching. I leave Baghdad for Basra on my way to Kunji Zagh.

Chapter 15 : *Basra to Bombay*
The three disciples of the Shah. Sufism decoded to mean 'Wisdom of the Divine'; religion a secondary manifestation of something higher. The activity seen as residing within the whole community. Difficulty of knowing right from wrong; people seeing a chrysalis demand to know where the butterfly is. 'A miracle to one man is commonplace to another'; the 'hidden correspondence' between worldly and other things.

Chapter 16 : *Amu Daria – The River Oxus*
I become a Mullah. Journey with Mirza as an expert on the *Five Jewels*. The Sufi 'banking system'. The Oxus people; four different Amu Daria communities visited. The patchwork cloak. Special gymnastics. How Pir Turki held up an army 'by the power of his glance'. Farming and distribution of profits. Prescience in the matter of the cooking-pot. The concept of 'self-work'. The great Jan-Fishan Khan. The consummation of this philosophy in the West.

Chapter 17 : *Stray Days*
Khoja Imdad and recollections of the Boxer Rebellion. When can a lie be the truth? Account of a teaching journey to an Indian town. Ideas about the 'Russian experiment'; the Sufi hero of the Caucasus. The man who travelled to America.

Chapter 18 : *Into Kafiristan*
On pony-back into Kafiristan. Descriptions of the region; the mountain demon. The descendants of Alexander the Great. The village, the wooden effigy of Gysh the Kafir god; resemblance to 'merrie England' the visit of Christian monks. Meeting with the Red Father. Back to Pakistan.

AMONG THE DERVISHES

CHAPTER ONE

Among the Dervishes

The pilgrims came to Karachi in their thousands; Indians, Pakistanis, stern Pathan giants from the North-West Frontier, tiny slant-eyed people from the further reaches of Kashmir. Men, women, children, with a fair sprinkling of ancient patriarchs who hoped, above all, that they would find their last repose during the journey to that far-off Arabian sanctuary, to visit which they had probably scraped together their savings, coin by coin, for decades.

Every year saw them come. We saw them, as we worked in stuffy offices, saw them come and go : saw them returning with the coveted title of *Haji,* perhaps with a tiny scrap of the *Kaaba's* curtain, or a tin of water from the *Zemzem* holy well. They went – and still go – by overpacked pilgrim ship, by private chartered aircraft, even on foot. Overland they follow the grim route of sunbaked Baluchistan, to Iraq, Jordan and thence southward through the parched Hejaz to – Mecca.

Although my mother, in a moment of poetic delight, had named me after the great Khayyam, I was not able to count myself among the Faithful; and, like many another infidel before, something inside me said that in spite of the interdict against the unbeliever, there must be a way to gain entry into the most forbidden city on earth. No unbeliever, (so said the Prophet thirteen hundred years ago) shall be allowed to pass the great portals of the Holy of Holies.

I enquired from the local Saudi-Arabian authorities. They were very correct and most polite. Yes, I could apply for a visa to visit Saudi-Arabia. No, it would not be possible for me to enter Mecca; although I might go as far as Jeddah, fifty miles away.

My first name, surely, was a Moslem one? The name 'Burke', was it derived from Barq, the Arabic word for lightning? Was I perhaps of Moslem extraction? No, I had to tell the official; I was half Scottish and half Irish. He was not without a sense of humour: 'Celtic? I would have taken you for an Englishman.' Then, in a more serious tone, which showed that, for all the modernity of today's Arabs, the Old Testament mentality dies hard, he continued, 'You *are,* of course, of Moslem origin. According to Islam, all people are born Moslems. It is their parents who make them into something else.' But this was not a sufficient ground to permit me to visit Mecca.

Faced with a problem such as this, and no local knowledge whatever, there was a temptation to drop the project altogether. Little by little, however, a picture began to form. Numerous talks with Moslem friends, especially those who had made the coveted journey, gave me the background knowledge that I needed. Assuming that I went as far as Jeddah, I would not be able to get to Mecca because my presence there would be known. I would have to stay at an hotel, and my identity as an unbeliever would be apparent. No Moslem, they all agreed, would connive in any attempt to smuggle me into the Holy City. I would stick out like a sore thumb, even in Jeddah. There had been attempts to gain entry to the city, and as a result the Saudi guards were very much on the alert. I spoke very little Arabic. I knew a good deal of Urdu, and some Persian, and had black hair and brown eyes. The last-named facts were about the only ones in my favour.

But what if, with my oriental-sounding names, I were to go as a Moslem? This was risky, thought my advisors, and all of them made it plain that they would not welcome such a thing, nor allow themselves to discuss it. And as a convert? Well, my friend Abdul-Samad had seen a Western convert (he did not know of what nationality) in Jeddah, who had been kept there until the Wahabi brethren, who make up the royal family's supporters, might be satisfied that he was sufficiently orthodox and real in his beliefs. When Abdul-Samad saw him, he had been waiting three years.

I certainly did not have as much time as that: for my job would allow me at the most three months' leave. Then fate stepped in. I received news that a legacy which had been pending was larger than I had expected, and decided to throw up my job. If it was not to be Mecca, it could be a protracted journey through some of the less-known parts of Central Asia – up the

Khyber, perhaps, and into the strange land of Afghanistan: a neighbouring country, whose enigmatic people were looked upon with a mixture of respect and fear by the gentler folk of Pakistan.

Not long after my good news, I sat in a teahouse where my Pakistani friends used to gather and eat *jelabies* and other sticky-sweet confections, going through a passage of one of the simpler of the Persian classics and turning over in my mind the possibilities beyond the beckoning ranges to the north-west, I saw a stranger eyeing me, narrowly I thought. He called for a water-pipe, adjusted his turban and leant across the rough table in my direction. I looked more carefully at him. He was small, with neat hands and feet, pale-skinned and wearing a tight turban and flowing robe of the wide-sleeved Persian pattern. In his right hand he held a string of beads. I must have been in a semi-reverie, because I started when he said, in a soft version of the Hindustani which is the lingua franca of Pakistan:

I said, 'Do you know the Chapter of the Manners of Dervishes?' I had been rehearsing a part of the First Chapter of the Rose-Garden of Saadi, a mystical poet of Persia, and my new friend evidently was a student of this literature.

His name was Akhund Mirza, he told me, from a family of Bokharan refugees who had in pre-Soviet days served the Emir across the Oxus. He was a Sufi, a follower of the way of life which Saadi extolled, and whose members form a freemasonry throughout the Moslem East. I told him my name, to which he remarked, '*Mikael* (Michael) is the name of an angel; and Omar was one of us.' For years I had wanted to know something about Sufism from the lips of a Sufi, and this was my chance. I had read a good deal about it in reference books, but had always thought that such of its poetry as I have seen did not accord with the definitions given of it. I could not believe, for instance, that it was merely the heretical or mystical form of Islam. And it turned out that I was right – and wrong.

'The Path of the Sufi,' said the Akhund, '*is* Islam, and it is not Islam. It is religion and it is not religion. This is because Sufism is the reality within all religion. How can one distinguish between one religion and another? You cannot compare the different kinds of milk by tasting the butter which they make.'

Sufism, he told me, was a way of life which was said to have been handed down from remote antiquity. Its procedures were designed to produce the perfected man – or woman. In order to achieve this, the Sufi had to go through a long training. The difference between this teaching and all other spiritual systems was that the Sufi training took place within the world, and not out of it. In fact, the Sufi disciple carried out his studies during his normal work, and his everyday life. This concept was new to me, and I begged Akhund Mirza to tell me more.

'If you are a free man,' he said, 'I will tell you more.'

'Why a free man?'

'Because I am leaving soon for a journey to my Sufi Circle, and I cannot remain here to talk to you.'

I made arrangements to travel with him the following day. It took very little time to pack the essentials of kit, to lend my flat to a friend, and to stock up with rupees from my new-found store. Then the Sufi and I, for all the world like a teacher and disciple of old, bent our steps towards Baluchistan. The difference between this journey and a traditional one was that we travelled by motor-lorry, the local substitute for buses, and listened to radio news-bulletins and recorded music at almost every stop where a cafe was to be found.

The Akhund – the word means 'holy man' – had been to Mecca, and he gave me the name and approximate address ('In the middle-sized *Suk*') of a compatriot in Jeddah, whom I might look up if I were ever to go there. He too, followed the Sufi Way. I noted the identification-signal of all Sufis. The Akhund greeted his confrères wherever he went with the Arabic word *Ishq* (love); and received the reply, *Baraka, ya Shahim* (Blessings, O my King!)

Three days of stopping and starting, of breaking down in desolate gulleys and adding a few strands of wire to what already looked like a mechanic's nightmare of an unserviceable truck, and we emerged from sunbaked, dust-laden, glaring road into a more fertile land. Greenery appeared, the flocks of sheep and goats by the wayside were less emaciated, the trees seemed taller, the land opened out into wider plains watered by rivulets trickling down from the uplands which we were ascending.

The driver of our atrocious vehicle, a one-eyed opium-smoker who looked as if he was a refugee from a blood-feud (and probably was) sang loudly and tunelessly, for he was nearing home. The mountains of dour Afghanistan were to our north, and our driver was taking through some contraband. Before turning towards his homeland, however, he was to deposit us near to the monastery of the Sufis.

Three days . . . it seemed, at times, like three hundred. But at last, with a screeching of what brakes he had left, the driver triumphantly drew up near a mark on a rock wall, which had evidently been there for generations, but which he greeted as if it was some rare and interesting discovery.

He would take no money from the Sufi, asking only for his blessing. Then, for good measure, he got mine as well. 'May you never be tired! May your sons be brave! May you be ever strong!' And the cheerful, reckless smuggler was shooting up the road, concentrating, no doubt, upon the latest methods of out-witting the sentries of the God-Bestowed Kingdom of the Af-ghans, their Allies and their Dependents. He would be back by the same route, if Allah willed, in a month. It was as good, almost, as an omnibus service. Akhund Mirza explained that a white flag was put by the road if any Sufi wanted a lift east-ward; a green one if he wanted to go westward. And the smug-glers and other drivers always hooted their horns and waited for the adept to appear.

At first there was no monastery in sight; no human habita-tion of any kind. This place, it seemed, was called *Kunji Zagh* – Raven's Corner. Neither corner nor raven was apparent while I was there.

Dusk was falling as we started up a narrow stony track, keep-ing to the right to avoid the very possible contingency of falling onto the road below. Out of training and very much out of breath, I was just reasoning that we must, at all events, be within earshot or hooter-distance of the road, when I realised that we were now going through a tunnel, and a man-made one at that. This was the entrance to the monastery, with a trickle of water passing along it : the mouth of a stream which formed a small waterfall lower down.

We turned a corner in the tunnel and saw, stretched like a string of pearls in moonlight, a wandering succession of tiny clay oil-lamps of Roman pattern reaching away into the dis-tance. Every dozen paces was a lamp, always to the left of the passageway, with its tiny glow-worm flame just perceptible as a reflection in the stream. Another curve, with the gradient getting steeper, and we were undoubtedly in a stone building, perhaps hewn from the inner matrix of the rock. In answer to my unspoken question, the Akhund said:

'When anyone wants to attract the attention of a vehicle passing below, he places his flag there, and sits and waits there. But this is the end of the climb.'

We were in a fairly large room, bare of all furniture and lit by a large lamp, of the bulbous, ornamented kind which one sees in mosques. This was the ante-chamber of the monastery, to which entrance was gained only through a slit, low down in the wall at the end of the chamber. An ideal place to defend, and an equally suitable way to impress any visitor with a sense of mystery.

Before wriggling through the slit, the Akhund called a salutation in a reedy voice: *'Yaaa-Hu!'* – and motioned me to follow him. We were now in an even larger room, well lit by a succession of mosque-lamps with huge rounded glass shades. In the centre of the room were two immense wooden tables. Around the walls were inscriptions in the monumental calligraphic style of the Arabic of Kufa, dating from about the eighth century A.D. One wall was bare, except for a sign representing the *Qibla* – the direction of Mecca towards which prayers are always said. This symbol exactly resembles the Greek letter Omega.

Sitting on sheepskins, with their legs folded under them, backs against the wall, were some thirty men, contemplatives of the monastery. Each was dressed in what looked like a patchwork quilt; the *khirqa,* robe of the Sufis; a mantle which is presented to the disciple by his teacher when he attains the degree of adept.

We advanced, and took the hand of each man in turn. In the centre of the row sat the Supreme Guide – the *Kalan Murshid,* chief of the community, a tall and dignified figure who welcomed me in Persian.

The monastery, he explained, had a shifting population, and was something between a retreat and a training-school. In addition to the contemplatives, there were some fifty disciples and an equal number of affiliates: people who were attending a course of instruction, as it were. Strangers, whether Moslem or otherwise, were not encouraged, for the Sufis were 'not understood' by the world at large.

I spent just under a month at this *Khanqa,* and gradually an impression of the meaning of Sufism built up. In retrospect it is possible to see how this was done by the artistic combination of sermons, dialogues, question-and-answer, and exercises. There is little wonder that the narrow clerics of orthodox Islam of the two main schools of thought dislike this strange body of men. In the first place, they preach the equality of the sexes, the fact that all relationships are based upon love, and they contend that no man can be the holder of another's conscience. They have little time for organised religion, because, they say, it lends itself too much to the domination of one man over another. When I mentioned that the disciple has to take an oath of absolute obedience to his teacher, I was told that this oath was but the prelude to setting free the learner : not a device to bind him to the Order.

I was allowed to be present, sitting in a circle on the battlements of the monastery, at the reception of a novice :

'Do you, Adan Adil, swear to obey the Order, the Chief of the Order, and the Highest Truth, obedient in the hands of your teacher as the corpse is submissive in the hands of its washers, until you in your turn become a teacher?'

'I swear.'

Then there was the question of discipline and self-mortification. The Sufi must be disciplined, I learned, but the austerities which he practises must be balanced by an equal amount of self-expression in the normal social world. He must have a secular vocation. The system in some ways was strongly reminiscent of the monastic orders of Europe in the Middle Ages : with the difference that there was this insistence upon taking part in ordinary life.

How was the Order organised? The chief explained this to me during one of our evening meals of roast lamb and spiced rice, which we ate in the open under the stars, when the nights were warm. 'All Sufis, we believe, are linked by a subtle force, which we call *baraka* (blessing). There is a hierarchy, but it is invisible after the grade of Murshid. The guiding principle is hidden within its host : the common mind of mankind.' There was one exception. On this earth the 'High Mantle' of Sufi supremacy devolved upon a member of the existing body of the descendents of Mohammed, for he it was who passed on the secret teachings of Sufism to a chosen circle. Sufism was the inner discipline of all religion, brought by all the Prophets, including, I was told, Jesus.

In addition to knowing the theory of Sufism, the members have to carry out the practices. First, meditation upon a theme set them by their teacher in accordance with his assessment of their needs; secondly, deep contemplation, to increase their powers and abilities. Finally there are the group exercises, of which the dancing of the dervishes is one form. Why, I asked, did we hear of the dervishes as wonder-workers, and mendicants, and not so much as philosophers and men of action?

'The ones whom you see,' said the Murshid with a smile, 'are those who are most perceptible to you. Each one who whirls in ecstasy or who can pick up red-hot irons is matched by a dozen who carry on the work. Or the same man may be, at other times, indistinguishable from other members of society because he is not carrying on these practises continuously.'

One remarkable exercise was carried out by all members of the fraternity. At intervals during the day, when Sufis might be coming and going, or carrying on various allotted tasks, the Murshid would appear and suddenly shout the command *Quiff!* Literally this means 'Stop!', and stop they literally did. Everyone froze in his tracks until the word *Hu!* was given. During the period of 'freezing', the meditation of the Sufi Point of View, as it is called, was taking place. The theory behind this is that when a person is at an intermediate stage between one action and another, he can free himself from the limitations of the ordinary thought-processes, which are held to be a barrier to concentration. I took part in this exercise in common with the rest.

The litany, called the *Zikr* (remembering) was held every night for an hour, and for the whole night preceding Friday. It consisted of a series of meditations, concentrations and repetitions of words and phrases. Sometimes there was music : the high wail of the reed flute and the drum; sometimes there was no accompaniment. And on Friday afternoons were held the 'healing sessions', when the whole community would concentrate upon improving, telepathically, the curative powers which wandering or other absent members of the colony were said to be exercising in a far-flung ministry. Courses of healing dramatically resembled hypnotic procedures, coupled with a form of laying-on of hands, in much the same manner as that of the old mesmerists.

About the supernatural beliefs of the Sufis I was able to learn little. As I was not an initiate I was excluded from some of their group meetings at which certain exercises were carried out. Popular belief credits Sufis with such powers as telepathy, prescience and miraculous transportation from one place to another. In the various books of the Sufis which were read out aloud from time to time in their daily assemblies, there was a good deal of poetry. There were many aphorisms, and much material on the lives of past Sufis.

Few of the more established dervishes would talk to me in the terms in which I was trying to ask questions. They were not very interested, for instance, in the history of Sufism except in any part of its story which might have a bearing on what they called 'the present task'.

Adan Adil, however, who was accepted into the community during my visit, was still full of the 'exterior' interest in the Sufi cult which characterised my own approach.

He had travelled very widely, into Soviet Central Asia, at great risk to himself; to Armenia and remote parts of Persia, as far West as Bulgaria and Albania, seeking factual Sufi lore.

I asked him why one should be a Sufi.

'Primarily if you feel an indescribable affinity with the Sufi folk, which you express in ways satisfying to your false self. This means, you may like Sufis or their literature, and you may think that these offer a good community for you or an attractive way of life. But what is really attracting you is the bell which rings within you. This is the answer to the Sufi call. This "answerer" was planted in you the moment you were created.'

I said that I found this hard to believe. He laughed, his weather-beaten Tatar face crinkled. 'Hard to credit, but you believe it already. You will not allow your priceless thinking apparatus to accept it, in case you think yourself credulous. You are in a mess, my friend.'

'But if you will not allow me to study Sufism in the only way I *can* think, how can I rely on some form of thinking which you tell me I have, yet which I have never had any evidence for?'

'The kind of evidence you need is a special kind. You have to get used to using mental muscles which are, at the moment, lax.'

But why should Sufism be so important? Did it claim to be a sort of human need, or something which would solve the problems of mankind?

'Yes. Many thousands of years ago, something went wrong on this planet. Man lost the power to raise himself from his lowly state to the one which is his destiny. Many people came, from time to time, to remind man of his high destiny. They were nearly all persecuted. Some of the messages are still preserved, in a more or less distorted form. These are the men – and the women – who have brought admonitions and methods for man to free himself from his fallen state, so that he can start to climb again. These are known in many languages as prophets. Your own great Jesus was one of them. He is one of our Masters. To you, he is merely the signal for the outpouring of emotions. For him you love, for him you kill. Through him you can no longer develop, for you have forgotten the vital part of his message.'

After that outburst, Adan never spoke to me again, though why I am not certain.

CHAPTER TWO

Solo to Mecca

Twenty-eight days had passed in this unfamiliar company when Akhund Mirza suggested that I might care to return with him to Karachi : for the one-eyed driver would be coming this way again soon, and I might like to carry on my life 'in the open air'. Returning by the same route, thankful that our smuggler had come back safely, we made the return trip.

The Akhund was silent for most of the time, and I did not try to converse with him, for the germ of an idea was maturing in my mind. I now had some idea of the ways of the Sufis, and I had learned that their communities existed far and wide within the Mohammedan world. I had learned a good deal about them, had even been treated in some ways as a disciple. I had the name and the address of a Sufi in Jeddah, the gateway to Mecca. All I needed now was to get to Jeddah, and thence find some method of entering the holy city.

Akhund Mirza supplied the link. When I asked him how to get to Saudi-Arabia, he mentioned that he had a friend in Port Sudan, just across the Red Sea from Jeddah, and that this man was a kind of pilgrim agent. Pilgrims from central Africa could, through his good offices, often get across the sea for less than it would cost by ordinary means. He knew the captains of fishing dhows. I shall call him Mutawassit, though that is not his real name.

If I were able to slip across the Red Sea, I reasoned, and into Saudi-Arabia without passing through the Foreigners' Control Office, I might be able to blend with the pilgrim throng and penetrate the fifty miles inland to Mecca. The Akhund's friend in Saudi-Arabia, might even give me a bed, thus avoiding the need to stay at an hotel. It seemed worth trying.

Three weeks and three changes of aircraft later, I was in Port Sudan. I had worked out certain rules for myself, in order not to lose my amateur status. I would use my real name, refer

to my sojourn in the Sufi monastery, make use of the name of
the Akhund, but I would be noncommittal about my nationality and origins. Port Sudan, pleasant place though it undoubtedly was, paled, even in reality, when measured against the
glamour of the forbidden Hejaz a few short miles eastward. It
was neat and trim, less exotic than the Arab lands, hot if not
so dusty, largely peopled by people of a distinctly Nubian cast
of feature. Like the faces in Egyptian frescoes. I took a room in
a white-painted hotel with bright green shutters, and explored
the town. Among the strolling afternoon crowds I glimpsed
many an Indian or Asiatic face, and most of them seemed to
head, eventually, for a row of shops in an arcade, shops selling
saris and incense and souvenirs and all the things that Indians
and tourists delight in. Here, sitting cross-legged in his palm-
beach suit, sweating profusely and mopping his lean face. I
found Mutawassit the general merchant, genial and friendly.

I bought a fan, fanned myself with it, told him my name and
mentioned that I knew the good Akhund, the holy man, and had
recently stayed with him. Mutawassit was delighted. What could
he do for me? How was his friend? Was he coming this way
again soon? From his accent I realised that he was a Pathan,
one of the wandering type who are to be seen all over the East,
and who eventually return to their crenellated village homes in
the border area and buy land, to become prominent local citizens. Meanwhile, Mutawassit Khan was a business man, anxious
to turn a rupee or two . . .

'I want to get on a boat, to Saudi-Arabia,' I told him. The
Pathan looked around. *'Koi pursopal hai?':* which in Hindustani
may be roughly translated as meaning 'Are they after
you?' I laughed, partly with relief. I had forgotten that the
frontiersman's first reaction to an approach of this sort would be
that there must be some urgent reason for a person wanting to
move : especially to the inhospitable wastes of the Hejaz. Danger
is meat and drink to the Pathan clansman.

Partly, I admit, in order to indulge a preposterous taste for
conspiracy, and partly to prevent, if possible, further questions,
I showed him the Sufi belt which the Murshid had given me as
a parting gift. As soon as he saw the octagonal buckle under my
jacket, Mutawassit stiffened. *'hukam farmaye'* – 'Order me,'

Mutawassit was an old hand at illegal immigration. His

underground network into Saudi-Arabia dated from the days
of the pilgrim tax, when the Wahabis charged each pilgrim
thirty pounds sterling for landing on their hallowed soil. Many
found it cheaper to take the 'Mutawassit line' than to use more
conventional means of transport. Had Mutawassit been in the
slave trade as well? Absolute nonsense, he told me. Journalists
from several Western newspapers had once descended upon
Port Sudan and questioned almost everybody, after an article
appeared somewhere stating that the Saudis got black slaves
by this route.

'If they do,' he said drily, 'they fly them in by chartered
planes. They have the means, and they use hired aircraft for
everything else.'

So far, so good. Mutawassit told me to equip myself with a
bush shirt, sandals and slacks. This, it seemed, was the standard
dress in Saudi-Arabia. Over this outfit the flowing Arab robe
was worn, as well as the white head-cloth and black head-
band: the 'Oqal and Kuffiyeh'. He gave me a small embroidered
skullcap and told me to stop shaving, but to have my hair cut
short.

'Don't speak Persian there,' he warned, 'the Persians are
considered to be heretics, they don't like them.' He never asked
what nationality I was. When I mentioned that there was
someone in Jeddah who would help me, Mutawassit realised
that this was Abdallah, because he referred to him as Alif-Lam:
the first and fifth letters of his name. I did not quite understand
at first that this numerical code was used, and it only struck
me when Mutawassit referred to himself as 'Meem-Soad' –
also the first and fifth letters of his name.

It was another fortnight before a sailing was announced, and
my beard was growing respectably: so was my knowledge of
Sudani Arabic. I had to go to the harbour and meet a rowing
boat, which would take me to another ship. As I left him,
Mutawassit pressed five golden sovereigns, of Queen Victoria's
minting, into my hand, wrapped in a piece of cloth.

'Art thou returning?'

'If Allah wills.'

In a few minute I was on a fishing boat, a crazy, leaking
affair which stank of jellyfish and was manned by three of the
blackest looking Arabs I have ever seen. Midgets of Hadhrami

stock, they wore only colourful loincloths and swore incessantly as their unpalatable craft, *The Resplendent One,* lurched across the dark waters through the velvety night, listing and tacking, and making their single passenger feel less sanguine about the great adventure when he remembered that Red Sea fishermen are reputed to push hapless pilgrims ashore on uninhabited islands – to return, when they have starved to death, for the purpose of rifling their effects.

After an age, it seemed, we ran ashore on a soft bank, and I was helped onto the hallowed soil of the Hejaz.

'May your life be long! O Sheikh, walk for half an hour in that direction, and thou shalt see the lights of Jeddah. With faith in Allah!'

I gave the captain a sovereign, and started my hike. I had no luggage save a cloth-wrapped bundle containing my documents and Egyptian currency notes, for the Saudis had not yet compromised with the West to the extent of printing their own money. In very much less than the promised half hour I did indeed see the blaze of lights which mark Jeddah: the town whose name means Ancestress, because tradition has it that Mother Eve herself is buried here.

My watch showed that sunrise would be in an hour, and I felt that it would be unwise to enter the town before that time. I had nowhere to go, and for all I knew there would be police patrols in the streets. I could never have accounted for my presence. But it was terribly cold in the desert, and no shelter was in sight. There was no moon, and I could feel no road underfoot: only the hard sand which surrounds the city. Then I heard a dog bark, far away, it was true, but an indication that I should not get within scent of it.

I remembered that Arabs were reputed to dig a hollow in the sand and sleep in it. But the sand seemed too hard. Patting around with my hands, I found a dune, the stand softer than anything that I had known since the sandpits of my childhood holidays. I discovered that I could insinuate myself into the pile, snuggling down for all the world as a tramp might in a haystack.

I lay facing Jeddah, strangely calm, as if some primitive instinct told me that I was safer here, half-buried, and thought about the hour and the days of reveries in which I had seen myself inside Mecca. Never, I reflected, had I visualised myself like an animal in a burrow, and a very impermanent one at that. This was more like an escape story from the War : a sort of escape in reverse : or perhaps the escape part was to come later. What were Saudi prisons like? Then I drifted off to sleep, and dreamt that I was being hunted by Saudis with dogs, but could not get way, because we – Saudis, hounds and me – were lurching around in a foul, leaking fishing-boat somewhere in the Red sea.

The heat of the sun woke me. It was well after sun-up. Parched and feeling rather dizzy, I reached for a cigarette, then remembered that smoking was said to be forbidden in Saudi-Arabia. Jeddah was easily visible, a cluster of stone houses, some of them with several stories, some modern buildings, less than a mile away. I shook off as much powdery sand as possible and set off for the city of Eve.

Jeddah is not walled, but straggles around the modernised port, a jumble of the very old and the very new. I noted that the town petered out into a series of long-abandoned, tall and shuttered Arab houses. Among them the only moving things were ungainly goats restlessly climbing the mounds of fallen masonry in search of seedlings. Wandering into the maze of deserted streets in this southern section of the city, I began to feel the real effect of heat. The sun beat down and seemed to be reflected from every wall. Due, perhaps, to my thirst, I found that I had lost my way, and ended up studying the same goat that I had seen several minutes before. I decided to march upon a crooked minaret, and soon came upon streets in which people walked to and fro, donkey-carts carried loads of miscellaneous goods, shrouded women shuffled past plate-glass windows where tractors and groceries were displayed. Nobody looked at me, and I felt reassured.

Just behind the largest of these Western-style streets I came upon the noisy, bustling entrance to the great *Suk* – and just beyond it my goal, the 'middle-sized' *Suk*. Open-fronted shops, little more than man-made caves, were piled with a profusion of merchandise, from plastic toys to amber beads, *Kabobs* roasting on spits, to bales of Kashmir cloth. It took two turns of the market street before I found Abdallah, sitting behind a pile of shoes and sandals of every kind, drinking his morning cup of coffee, his little slanted Uzbek eyes and scanty beard giving him the appearance of an enigmatic gnome. Just above him, hung in a frame of silver, was the inscription 'The Shoes of Abdallah, son of Yusuf, El-Bokhari'. It was written in black, upon a background of terra-cotta : the Sufi colour, which distinguishes many Sufi houses in the East.

Abdallah came forward when I stopped at the entrance, and invited me in, had his boy bring a cup of coffee, and started to talk in Arabic. In a mixture of Arabic and Persian (the latter being his mother tongue) I told him that I was a friend of Akhund Mirza, that I brought his salutations, and that I sought somewhere to stay. Without hesitation, he led me to a room above the shop, furnished with a string bed, a pitcher of cool water and a prayer-rug. 'You are my guest, please do not leave us.'

Abdallah and his two adolescent sons were charming people, remarkably cultivated for shoemakers, and very interested in the world outside. I told them that I wanted to make 'the Visit' to the Mecca Sanctuary, that I wanted to do it as soon as possible, and that I would then travel onwards. 'When I was twenty years younger,' said Abdallah, 'my spiritual director also sent me on such a journey : to China, and I derived great benefit from it, though I did not at first realise its significance.' His elder son, Murad Ibn Abdallah, would take me to the Holy City and bring me back. Would I like to go that afternoon?

I had hardly bargained for things working out so well, and I told Abdallah so. 'When an intention is genuine, all doors open,' he said. After a meal of rice cooked with butter and strips of meat – Bokharan rice, as the dish is called by the Saudis – I retired to rest in my room. Three hours later, Abdallah woke me up, and showed me my pilgrim garb. Two large bathtowels had been bought, and I was taught how to twist one around my middle, like a sarong, and throw the other over my shoulders, leaving one arm bare. On my feet were to be new sandals, and I was told to be in a state of ritual purity, which included having a bath and a shower. The pilgrim was not allowed to carry anything of a secular nature, nor to wear anything on his head. Written down on a scrap of paper was the invocation which I had to repeat while I set off with the 'high intention' of accomplishing the Visit :

Solo to Mecca

Labbayk Allahumma, Labbayk!
Labbayk: La sharika-lak, labbayk!
Inna al-hamda wa an'niamata la-ka w'al mulk:
La sharika-lak!

'Here am I, O Allah, here am I! Thou without partner, here am I! Verily all praise and graciousness is Thine: and all sovereignty. Indivisible One!'

Murad and I set out in our white, shroud-like garments, just as the sun was going down and the muezzin's cry broke forth from Jeddah's minarets: 'Come to prayer, come to success!' Parked just off Faisal Street, the main thoroughfare, was a large shooting-brake, already packed with people, all in pilgrim white. They were residents of Jeddah, upon whom the pilgrimage is, of course, just as obligatory as upon other Moslems.

Almost every day, I was told, parties of people would club together to hire a car and drive to the Forbidden City, and avoid the expense of employing one of the professional *Mutawwifs,* pilgrim guides authorised by the Government to lead the faithful through the ceremonies. I was glad that we were in a private party, for pilgrims are grouped according to nationalities, and whatever nationality I had pretended to be, a Mutawwif would undoubtedly have seen through me. As it was, Murad and his father showed no interest in my origins, in true Sufi manner.

As evening fell we headed out of Jeddah along the broad black ribbon of the macadamised road, travelling over the wonderful surface at over sixty miles an hour, chanting our litany and feeling almost in another world. The car swept past the winking lights of the huge palace of the capitalist Ba-Khashab Pasha, transport king of the Hejaz, looking exactly like a wedding cake with pale green icing. By the side of the road, walking, riding horses, mules, donkeys camels, moved the more conventional pilgrims, taking advantage of the cool of the evening for their first sight of the holy of holies: though they would have to camp overnight at the halfway halt where King Ibn Saud had built shelters for the faithful. Few vehicles were coming from the direction of Mecca. An occasional police-car, loaded with fierce-looking gendarmes in khaki with green headcloths: several most imposing Cadillacs and Mercedes, with the crossed-swords and palm-tree badge of the Royal Transport Unit, a few lorries loaded to the utmost with baggage of returning pilgrims. The road is straight for most of the way, running across a plain where nothing moves and nothing grows, save a few desert shrubs, occasionally glimpsed in the headlights.

None of my companions spoke to me during the journey : or to one another, for that matter. Gripped with religious fervour, they repeated their prayers and dedicated themselves to the object of the journey.

After nearly thirty miles, when we reached the half-way halting place, the plodding mass of pilgrims thinned out until we had the road almost to ourselves.

The new moon was a thin, low sickle in the sky. So clear was the air that the stars seemed to hang like glowing fruit, eerily just above our heads. Now outcrops of yellow and reddish rock were to be seen in our headlamps, and the road swept upwards into the Mecca hills, nothing more than a saffron gap clawed by man through igneous rock. Then down again, more precipitately this time, and almost before I knew it, we were through the huge gateway of the city, and edging through tens of thousands of pilgrims who choked the streets. Suddenly the car stopped, and I saw a man with *Sharta* (Police) on his shoulder-strap looking into the car. He exchanged a greeting with some of the occupants, whom he evidently knew, and we were allowed to proceed.

'Stick with me,' whispered Murad, as the station-wagon again stopped, apparently in an ordinary street. We all piled out, and I followed Murad and the rest of the throng through an enormous gateway where a gimlet-eyed Wahabi policeman with a cane in his hand was conning every face as pilgrims jostled each other to enter the Holy Shrine. This was the Gate of Abraham, who reputedly rebuilt the Grand Mosque as a pious act. Three more steps and we were within the Holy of Holies of all Islam.

The sight was really breathtaking. We had emerged beyond the massive wall into a narrow courtyard, then, with unexpected rapidity, the crowd moved through a gateway into a flagged arena of such size and impressiveness that the memory of St. Mark's Square in Venice paled before it. Beneath our feet were marble slabs, laid out in a pattern leading to the centre, where the huge bulk of the *Kaaba,* the cubical temple, loomed in its black covering. Embroidered in a wide band on the upper part of this edifice – the Shrine of the Black Stone – were golden verses from the Koran, which threw back the light shed by thousands of electric lights, artistically concealed throughout the arena.

Within the area were several erections. One was the praying-place of Abraham, another the cupola covering the Sacred Well Zemzem, which reputedly nourished Hagar, mother of Ishmael, when she was wandering in the wilderness. All around me, dwarfed by the immensity of it all, padded pilgrims of every hue, in every human shape and size.

Some of the pilgrims were alone, others in small parties led by Mutawwifs, circumambulating the Kaaba, sipping the miraculous water of Zemzem, some telling beads as they sat cross-legged before the Kaaba or in the cloisters which surround the square. Murad motioned me to follow him towards the Kaaba, with palms upraised as he repeated a prayer. As we reached the building, which is merely a huge granite-built cube, innocent of furnishings, from which Mohammed cast out the pagan idols of the pre-Islamic Arabs (and whose door is almost never opened) I realised that the famous Black Stone is actually set into an outside corner of the wall. The heavy black covering is slit at this point, so that the pilgrims may have access to the Stone. Following Murad, I placed my hands upon the shiny surface of the Stone, then kissed it, and continued with the ritual circuit of the Kaaba, which is carried out in an anticlock-wise direction. The press of pilgrims beside the Stone was considerable, and I was only able to note that it was set inside the granite, surrounded by a wide silver band, and that – unlike the marble underfoot – it was not cool to the touch.

After the sevenfold circuit we withdrew some distance from the Kaaba to say the Prayer of the Visit, and took a sip of water from a brass bowl proferred by one of the small boys who dispense it, and whose prerogative (because of their noble descent) this function is. The water tasted slightly alkaline.

As we sat down facing the Kaaba in meditation, I noticed the ubiquitous Wahabi policemen mixing with the crowds, swinging canes and looking occasionally towards the glass-fronted office, high up in one of the buildings around us, where the officials of the Administration keep watch on the sanctified area and flash lights in signal to their police below. There was no sign of religious ecstasy or abandonment: perhaps Saudi law forbids it; but there was a most perceptible atmosphere of devoutness such as has to be experienced, and cannot really be described.

The people taking part in this ritual were fulfilling one of the commandments (a 'Pillar') of Islam. They had been brought up to consider that nothing on this earth could exceed the merit which they would obtain by making the Visit to the Shrine. They were treading the very ground where the Prophet and his companions had walked: towards which over four hundred million souls daily turn five times in prayer.

Murad at length arose, touched my arm, and led me from the Sanctuary. The car was waiting, and within half an hour, with our full complement, we were speeding back to Jeddah. Abdallah asked me whether I had to go anywhere else, or whether I would wait for the next Sufi meeting, which was to be held in six days' time. I told him that I would prefer to take up my journey again, and that if it could be arranged I would like to be conveyed across the Red Sea again, to Port Sudan. 'Nothing easier' he said, and his sons took me to another fishing-boat rendezvous: and out of the magical world of Saudi-Arabia. And all by means of the world within a world which is of the Sufis. The Akhund had been right when he said, 'Sufism is being adapted to every contingency in every era.'

Mutawassit welcomed me back literally with open arms, and invited me to his home. He lived in an apartment above the shop, furnished in that rather self-conscious combination of chromium and polished wood which seems to attract the Indian trader abroad. He was very proud of his cuckoo-clock, his Bond-Street slippers, given him by a British customer, his plastic model of the Taj Mahal, illuminated from the inside by means of a battery and bulb.

As far as his spiritual studies went, he consorted with a small band of like-minded people, all interested in Sufism, who met in his 'silent room' each alternate Thursday.

This silent room was a very different proposition. It had a white Indian carpet, rugs of Central Asian pattern on the walls, and cushions scattered on the floor, Mutawassit and his Indian, Arab and Sudanese friends were no intellectuals. They would not have been able to read Rumi in the original, neither could they have made head nor tail of Ibn el-Arabi and his Sufi stanzas on divine love. They met, they talked, and there carried out the exercises of the Qadiri, Naqshbandi and Shadhili orders of Sufism, into all of which Mutawassit had been initiated.

The purpose of the Sufi activity, apart from helping others of the same persuasion, was considered to be 'service'. By keeping up the practises of the Orders, it was believed that the whole of the 'dervish work', throughout the world, was being helped. This 'service' was assumed to be something analagous to an electrical accumulation. When the time for individual salvation came, the Hidden Friends would send opportunities. Meanwhile there was – service.

When I had spent three weeks with these good people, and told them everything I knew about the Path, and heard what they could tell me, an opportunity arose. A tramp steamer was calling at the Port, en route for Alexandria. I was given an address in this town by the father of a student at the university there, and I decided to be on my way.

I spent most of my time during that voyage practising Arabic – of a sort – with the Somali crew, and straightening out my impressions. For there were many things about the 'dervish work' which hardly made sense. I also read and almost committed to memory the books on the history and practices of Islam which I had bought in Port Sudan.

Awfi-el-Sibri was the name of the Alexandrian student. He was a Sudanese by birth, his father having some agricultural land in the Gezira district. He had been sent to Egypt for secondary education, and was now reading history in Alexandria, with a view to an academic career.

I found him to be a boarder with a family of very orthodox Moslem divines, several of whom were graduates of Al Azhar university of Cairo, all of them deeply involved in the spiritual wellbeing of Egypt. Awfi was everything that they were not. There must have been nearly a dozen of them: short, grave, bearded, wearing the tiny fez, white turban and dark robe of the Azhar graduate cleric. None of them spoke English. The first thing each one of them wanted to know was whether I knew the Koran by heart, and whether there were any Christians left in England, because they had heard it said that the Islamic Cultural Centre in London had done such good work that 'masses' of people had been converted to Islam. Putting them right on that score did not endear me to them.

Awfi, on the other hand, was tall, thin, European-suited and lively. He loved the things of the East as well as of the West. But he had no time, though he never said so to their faces, for the pious rigmaroles of the scholars, his 'uncles'.

They, for their part, thought him odd. They could not accuse him of infidelity, Uncle Mustafa Munawwar informed me, but, well, there was something disturbing about the boy.

When he was not at classes, Awfi delighted in – as he called it – 'taking new experiences'. Only later did I find out that this was a part of the course prescribed for him by his Sufi teacher in Alexandria.

One day he said: 'How about becoming the first Englishman to attend a secret meeting of the Moslem Brotherhood?' I had heard – who had not? – of this fanatical politico-religious party, and jumped at the chance.

Awfi and I took a tram to the outskirts of Alexandria towards the time of the evening prayer, to a certain garden; something roughly equivalent to a common in England, I supposed. Although it was enclosed by a high wall, people were going in and out through the various gates in twos and threes, carrying what looked like picnic equipment and rations, mostly in small bundles. Most of these people were, it is true, young men, and much more alert in expression than the average Egyptian that I had seen in the metropolis.

The huge 'garden' was undulant, and Awfi guided me to a hollow in which about thirty youths and two or three older men – no women – were sitting in a circle. In their midst others were making preparations for a meal. We all shook hands, and every time anyone joined the group he, too, shook hands with everyone present.

Awfi now steered me to a sort of rockery upon which a solitary figure sat and introduced us.

'This,' he said to me, 'is Sa'eed Ramadan, Deputy Supreme Guide of the Moslem Brethren.'

Now the Brotherhood is severely proscribed in Egypt, and Ramadan was a wanted man. He had in fact been in Europe, via Pakistan to which he had fled during a purge of Brotherhood members. Now, it seemed, he was back at home, and quite in evidence. He spoke good English, welcomed me to the meeting, said that the suggestion that the Brethren were mad fanatics was vastly exaggerated, and offered me a cigarette.

He was in his early fifties, strong and lithe, with compelling eyes and a remarkable flow of words, even for an Arab, as I was soon to hear.

When the meal – roast meat, flat unleavened bread, onions and tomatoes – had been served and eaten, Ramadan spoke.

He started in almost a whisper, and I expected his voice, like that of many rabble-rousers, to rise until he was screaming. I looked around to see whether we could be overheard. It was obvious that the spot was well chosen, because in every direction there was a lookout posted, standing on a hillock. We could not be surprised.

Sa'eed Ramadan preached a sermon, strongly historical, in which he claimed that the events which had followed Egypt's independence had 'not been pursued in the spirit of religion.' Therefore, until a new leader appeared to guide the community – as the late martyred Sheikh Hasan el-Banna, Supreme Guide, had shepherded them – there would be no 'easement for Egypt, no recourse for her people, no light to shine forth as it shone forth to the nations in the past from here, our sacred land.'

The speech was well received. It was a nice mixture of politics, religious fervour and messianic expectancy.

Then Ramadan clapped his hands and, like genies from the Arabian Nights, we melted away. I melted with Awfi, who led me to a different gate, and we walked home in the cool of the evening.

The following day was Friday, when most Moslems took a day of rest, and Awfi took me with him for the *Ziara,* to pay his respects to his spiritual teacher, the Sheikh Hamad ibn al-Jabri, Sheikh of the Alexandria 'lodge' of the unified dervishes.

Although most historians deal only with individual orders of Sufis, these splinters are not in fact the main centres of Sufi activity. United congregations, their members drawn from several of the fraternities, are today's rule among the Sufis, whether of Arabia, Africa or Central Asia.

Sheikh al-Jabri was born in Tunisia. After attaining initiation into five or six Orders, he was finally accepted as a teacher of a 'unified lodge'. This *Zawiia* regarded itself as purged of the drawbacks of the personality-cult Orders and concentrated upon human self-improvement as a part of a combined effort.

It was in this company that I learned about the inner circle in Sufism. In the presence of strangers or members wedded to maintaining the name or identity of any particular Order, the members will behave as if they belong to that Order. They will use its hoary rituals, speak only of its venerated founder, wear its distinctive headgear. But when operating as an inner circle, the entire 'lodge' will revert to what they call the 'activity' of the original Way, sometimes called the Working of the Foundation, or Fundamental Work. This phrase is extremely difficult to translate, but because it can also mean such things as 'the work of the archetypes', which means in turn the group regards its activities as being identical with the parallel actions of an extra-terrestrial force which guides them.

Sheikh al-Jabri was learned both in the traditional lore of the Four Ways and also in modern methods of thought. Unlike the saintly type of North African mystic which is so common in the Great Maghreb, his earliest studies had been carried out in Europe, and had not been theological at all. It was only after he was thirty years old that he started to attend the great teaching centres of Kairawan and Mulai Idriss.

His father had been in Turkish service, and sent the boy to Paris, where he attended school and later the University of Paris. He had absorbed Western ways of thought and graduated in French literature. He knew a great deal of English, besides, because he was an import-export merchant carrying on a flourishing trade with Britain and the Commonwealth.

The Sheikh was married to a Lebanese woman, and his sons had attended the American University in Beirut.

He advised me to study not Sufism alone, but the attitudes, opinions and way of life of the people of the East and of the West. This, he said, was because otherwise I would simply equate Sufism with the East. I would not be able to descry the thread of Sufi thought and 'being' in both cultures unless I knew what was *not* Sufism.

'My son and brother,' he smiled, stroking his white beard and looking at me through brilliant Berber-blue eyes, 'too many Westerners become *orientalised*. This is sometimes because they seek spirituality in the East and think that therefore *everything* in the East is for them or can teach them something. Do not be like them.'

I asked him what, in the West, we could cultivate and emulate, in order to make our own tradition stronger. He gave me some strange examples. The first was team-spirit. This enabled man to understand what it was to work with others in harmony. The second was not democracy but a preparation for it. This enabled one to value democracy which itself was the prelude to understanding of the real equality of man. The third was respecting other people. This, he said, enabled one to respect oneself. 'But you cannot respect yourself unless you respect others. This is a great secret.'

I was to be very sure, he stressed, that I realised that all these three valuable secrets were points of development which were already deeply rooted in my own culture. It was for me to help them grow, to defend them, to work on them.

'Unless you have the three things in your heart, you are a hypocrite if you say that you are looking for a teacher.'

We had many talks, and I many times attended the sessions of the Sufis who were with Sheikh Jabri. One day he said to me :

'I cannot teach you, though you sometimes ask me, things which you demand to know . . . But I can help you towards learning some of these things, perhaps by an unfamiliar route. Are you ready to travel?'

Although I did not really want to leave this companionship I said that I was.

'Very well. See how life is for some of your fellow men. Go to Tunisia, see some friends of mine. Perchance you will see something about man through their eyes.'

This was how I came to make my way to Tunis.

CHAPTER THREE

Tunisian Caravan

Ours was a small caravan: thirty people and fifty animals between them was the average strength as we wound our way from Frenchified north Tunisia towards Nefta Oasis, Jewel of the Sahara and magnet for seekers after truth – members of the mystical Orders. We passed through the ruins of mighty North African sovereignty, where watch-towers told of emirs of the past intent upon preserving their land against the inroads of their neighbours. We plodded along stony highways which might well have been built by the Carthaginians; beyond the usual limits where Westerners in their shiny cars stopped briefly to drink in some breathtaking view of square towers and palm trees, then turned their wheels back to the neon lighting and very consciously Moorish decor of the capital's hotels.

Two men, the joint caravan-leaders, muffled in semi-Taureg fashion, pranced ahead on their wonderful Arab horses. At times they seemed to be swallowed by the rippling sand; sometimes they relapsed into near-immobility, riding like centaurs, and called by all the caravan 'The Cavaliers'. More than once, as we plodded along through the shimmering heat of August, they seemed to become divided into two; at other times they seemed to be walking upside down – effects of the true mirage which are so common that people take no notice of them at all.

Camels, donkeys and horses, these are the most important members of the caravan when it is on the move. And, when it stops, it is they who are looked after first. My camel was sulky, and seemed to be moulting in more than one place. She belonged to the deputy chief of the caravan, who was in charge of camping arrangements, and hoped to make enough profit from selling his wares at Nefta to provide his family with food for three months at the least. Beside me rode Si Hamid, who had attached himself to me soon after I landed in Tunisia, and without whom this journey would have been impossible.

Hamid was a half-Berber, and a priceless soul who lived by such things as cleaving to people of substance and working his fingers to the bone for them. His sponsorship gave me the entrée to many a household, whether tented or otherwise. Without sponsorship the East can be an empty place indeed. Although the Arab code of hospitality holds good here as elsewhere and no traveller is likely to be molested except by the outlaws who are in any case risks shared by all, he would achieve almost no contact with the unaccountable beings who pursue the Way of the Enlightened in their own, specific way.

Si Hamid's father had been a respected man, something of a recluse towards the end of his life, but still a name to be reckoned with. He was linked by marriage to several influential families, and in one way or another managed to preserve his unique way of life: a traveller without means, and a working one at that.

'Camels,' said Hamid, 'know the Hundredth Name of Allah. They are the only beings who know this, the most beautiful Name. That is why they look so haughty.'

I looked at him with some surprise. 'Hamid, I know that too. I think that everyone in the West, some of whom have not even seen a camel, know it too. I have read somewhere that nobody wants to be told this again. They are tired of it.'

'Art thou tired of it?' Hamid lapsed into the familiar form of speech.

I looked at his face. It bore the characteristic expression of the Easterner when he is about to impart knowledge. 'No, I am not really tired of it.'

'Very well, then. Among us, Sidi Omar, things are not said just because nobody has said them before. Would the language not become exhausted if everyone tried to say what men had not said before?'

'Yes, if you put it that way. But people get tired of the same thing.'

'Not *all* people. There are some sayings which we repeat because they have a meaning, and because the repetition of that meaning gives us something. Suppose, when you said, "Peace upon thee," I said, "I have heard that before?" Or, suppose, again, that you used a phrase and I said, "I have heard that before." What kind of speech could we have?'

'I did not intend to be discourteous. I only meant, perhaps, that I was looking for phrases and ideas which I had not heard before.'

His eyes brightened. 'That is different. That means that you want to enlarge your experiences and their depth. That is good.'

He looked straight at me, his round face and hazel eyes serious under the small tarboosh.

'Are we both happy now?'

We both laughed.

'Thank you for making me laugh,' said Hamid; 'have you heard *that* saying before?'

Hamid was in great demand as a story-teller when we made one of the daily halts. Men, women, children would gather around him as soon as he sat down; and the tale would always be one taken from the collections of stories used by the mystics. On this occasion, I determined to test his versatility by asking him to tell a story illustrating some aspect of our conversation.

'O Hamid! You had occasion to rebuke me today about my usage of words and my interest in phrases. What do you say, as a Seeker from among the Sufis, about this insistence of yours upon pedagogic matters?'

'I will tell you a story,' said Hamid at once, 'to redress the balance. Know, therefore, that life is composed of *ilm* (knowledge) and *aml* (action). You must balance the two. Here is the story, told originally by one of the great Masters, and told to me in similar circumstances by my own teacher. A grammarian, who was very pompous, had hired a small ship to take him on a journey. He asked the boatman as they sailed along, "Hast thou studied grammar?". And the man answered "No"; whereupon the scholar said: "Then you have wasted *half* your life." Soon afterwards a storm blew up, and the sailor said to the grammarian: "Hast thou learned to swim, O Sage?" – to which that worthy replied that he had not. "In that case" said the sailor, "*all* thy life is lost: for we are sinking!" '

As we moved southwards, now strung together as if by an invisible thread, now straggling over a fairly wide area as the trail widened, we passed here and there a white dome over the tomb of a marabout. 'Africa is covered with these marabouts', said Hamid. 'They give their sanctity out to the world. Each one of those graves marks sanctuary and freedom from arrest, as well as being a constant reminder of how we come and go in this life. We enter it crying, and yet we leave it crying also.'

One tomb was in a depression, where some water had managed to make its way to the surface, even to nourish a single palm tree. Beneath the tree several stakes were standing; from each one a number of knotted rags hung limply.

'Is it true that those rags are tied there as a reminder to the saint to help people who make a visit to the shrine, that he may help them in some supernatural way?'

'No,' said Hamid, 'You are wrong. Absolutely.'

'Then what are they for?'

'They are pieces of garments which have been worn by supplicants. The *baraka,* the inner power and blessing, of the sheikh who is buried in the tomb forms a link with the essence of the person whose garment this was. By this means the *baraka* is transmitted to the sufferer.'

'Irrespective of distance, and the time which has elapsed since the death of the sheikh?'

'That is so.'

'Where was I wrong?'

'You were wrong in thinking that they remind the sheikh of anything. They merely contact the *baraka* which suffuses the surroundings.'

'Are such prayers answered?'

'If Allah wills.'

There were two marabouts in the oasis where we stopped for the night-halt; set artistically on the gentle sloping side of a dry wadi, each with its tiny red-rag tokens, silent witnesses to the needs of many people. Under the deputy caravan-master the groups of travellers arranged themselves in the shade of the trees which grew without regard for pattern around the shrines.

Four ragged Negroes – the humblest members of our caravan – entered the precincts of the nearest building, raising their hands before the doorway, exactly as if warming them at a fire.

'They hasten to the *baraka*,' I said to Hamid.

'Yes, the *baraka* – and also the food. You see, in these parts pious travellers who pass this way leave provisions for the needy inside marabouts. There will be water, dates, perhaps some bread and even a coin or two. The rule is that each may eat as much as he thinks he may need until the next halt, but none may carry anything away.'

Two racy-looking camelteers, hardly stopping to munch their bread and hard-boiled eggs, took out a small drum and a flute and started to play a compelling rhythm, wailing at intervals to give their performance extra force. The austere, towering and very hawk-faced Senussi who was sitting near them rose to his feet and moved away to a spot just within the circle of our baggage, as far from the source of this accursed levity as he could be.

A harassed-looking little man settled his plump wife and two children in a hollow near the brackish spring and came over to us.

'I am about to call the prayer of sunset, and my name is Bou Hassan. When I call the "Rise to Prayer", who will be the Imam? As we do not all know one another, and our former prayer-leader has left the caravan, we must elect the man foremost in piety, you know.'

Hamid was silent; and I knew that he was not over-interested in this congregational problem. 'Ask the Senussi Sheikh' I suggested.

Bou Hassan fussed away to canvass support in conformity with custom, while we wolfed the meat balls which Hamid had obtained from somewhere, and tasted the tart sweetness of the fresh dates which I had brought. I went over to the spring to wash. There was only a trickle, for the water which had collected since the last caravan had been by now mostly used by people and animals. In the desert fashion, I rubbed handfuls of ochre, finest sand on my face, hands and feet. It made an excellent, only slightly abrasive, substitute for soap.

Then, through the bubbling roar of the camels, the crying of children and the mutter of conversation, the high calls of the muezzin cut into my consciousness: 'Come to prayer, come to success . . .'

Like a miniature army the faithful ranged themselves behind the Senussi, as Bou Hassan called out rapidly, like a sergeant-major, almost, 'Stand for prayer, stand for prayer.'

Dressing from the right, we formed three rows, facing the direction of the Kaaba in Mecca, across three-quarters of Africa, beyond Libya, the Sudan, the Red Sea coasts.

Rolled in my sleeping-bag I slept that night the sleep of exhaustion; for riding camels is not an easily acquired art.

When the harsh cry of the caravan-master in my ear told me that it was nearly dawn, I could hardly move. Stiff and sore, I groaned and felt that I would have to stay here at least a day to recover, come what may. But Hamid rolled me on the ground, and beat my body with his fists.

'It is an old trick,' he said, 'and generally one which has to be performed on fat merchants and soft women, unused to the ways of the desert, O Warrior!'

Ten minutes of this, and I was ready to march. Immediately after the dawn prayer we set off, deeper into the desert, munching dried dates and wetting our lips with water from goatskin bottles. Before the sun was fully up the desert air seemed charged with vitality, and we jostled one another as the whole caval-cade took up the choruses of the rollicking caravan-song, which means something like this: 'Let's go, let's go, we must be on our way; all hail, all hail, all hail to the Friend!' The Senussi ascetic bore this further discourtesy with fortitude.

At the halt before Nefta, I noticed a tall, erect figure on a well-caparisoned Arab swerve to a halt on a mound just above our watering-place. When I saw the glint of something reflecting the sun, I threw myself down on my face. There was a roar of laughter from the company.

'Brother,' said the Senussi, speaking his first words to me, 'it is but one of Hilali's warriors who spies us through a glass.' Hilali, according to Hamid, was the chieftain in whose lands we were. His man was counting heads, in order to levy a 'tax' upon the chief of the caravan.

Nefta Oasis is hardly a place for members of a conducted tour, especially if they want all modern conveniences. Yet it is soaked in the strange atmosphere of timelessness which makes one believe that there is a force somewhere around, waiting to be employed. More, much more, than Timbuktu – said Hamid – Nefta is the back of beyond.

Nestling in what seems from a distance nothing more than a series of Saharan sand-dunes, an island of green in an orange-yellow sea, it belongs to a really different world from the one which we normally know in the West. The people are proud, mysterious in their self-sufficiency; fighting-men as well as devotees of what can only be described as an occult school. Their oasis could well be the head-quarters of everything that opposes Western penetration. If a film company wanted to portray the traditional stronghold of the desert raiders, to which they return after yet another foray against the Foreign Legion, Nefta could be their model.

Outsiders are not welcomed here for any length of time, although caravans like ours wend their way into the sacred settlement without challenge. And sacred it undoubtedly is, for this is an important shrine of one of the branches of Senussism, the austere mystical system which numbers its followers in millions. Even today this cult provides the wellsprings of thought and action in a land where one would almost think that Nature had decreed that no man should live.

The palm trees give Nefta a surprising number of the things which the Arab needs: food, fibres, wool and shelter.

I could not have survived for long in this unco-operative place without Hamid. I wanted to see the Grand Sheikh of the Order, but I was uncertain as to his welcome, for my introduction was from a member of another community. I wandered around the sprawling oasis while Hamid, his plumpness somewhat hampering his movements, went to announce our arrival to the powers-that-be.

Nefta is often called The Pearl; and like a pearl it has grown with irritation, the constant impact of the caravans which pass through it. As a commercial centre, it has an entrepôt importance; and a middle-class element is seen from the clusters of small and undistinguished houses, rising from the very desert. But the praying-places of the dervishes – the Zawiyas – these are different. The mosques are simple, yet they show thought in planning, and their height produces a sense of coolness as well as majesty.

Muffled figures, wrapped up to exclude the heat of the early afternoon, were filing into a whitewashed Zawiya: four walls, with the tomb of their patron and teacher attached. Leaning against a rocky outcrop, roofed over, it was surrounded by cloisters. In contrast to the members of the north-bound caravan, merchants who looked at me with curious eyes, the mystics spared me no glance. There was no evidence of Western influence in sight, unless you could count the single word, written in Arabic script, on a bale of material in the doorway of a low-built shop. It said, simply : 'Teereeleen'.

'Nobody goes to Nefta,' they had said in the north. And it was true in the sense that nobody went there unless for a specific purpose. This has, of course, been said of Clapham Junction and Grand Central Station; but the atmosphere was very different from either of them. A caravan unhitching its beasts and wares, black-visaged central Africans offering their services as porters, dervishes winding their way like mediaeval friars to their zawiyas. But it seemed that anyone who came here just to see the place would find himself cut off by a barrier as impenetrable as any. The people simply did not want to know a stranger. You could look at the houses, at the open-fronted shops, the markets; at the palm trees and marabout domes. Social life? Tourist guides? Fizzy drinks? This was another world, and metropolitan Tunis seemed centuries away.

I sat down at a long table in the gloom of the suk, which evidently served as a café : asked for dates and water, and waited. Huddled figures sitting over their tea showed not the slightest interest; though a veiled Toureg with gimlet eyes near an empty hearth kept me under observation. I saw that he had two belts shining with cartridges strapped across his chest under the flowing mantle. In the centre of his stomach a silver-mounted disembowelling knife glittered as he moved to address a word to a one-eyed man who sat beside him, red hair sprouting from below the tarboosh crammed upon his immense head. This man was cleanshaven, and wrapped in a dark-brown hooded cloak, Moroccan slippers peeping from below its hem. He did not squat, but sat cross-legged. Then I saw that he was polishing a Mauser, and looking at it from time to time with every evidence of satisfaction.

'Desert raiders,' I thought. Hollywood would have snapped them up on the spot. Or were they a little over-played?

One-eye came over to me, and sat on a chair. *'Labas Alaik'* (May you be happy) he said. I returned the greeting, which has not changed during recorded time. 'Heinz Ringer, Captain,' he said, 'now Suleiman Ranjour. Who are you?'

I answered him in Arabic, not really wanting to find a language in which we were more fluent. 'I am a traveller.'

'Religious?' He looked at my clothes, travel-stained Arab ones, and at my simple repast.

'Averagely.'

'You are alone?'

'No, I am continuously attended by two guardian angels. At the same time they write down both my good and evil actions.'

There was very little that he could take from me, I thought, very little money. If he were to try to capture me for ransom I would appear to submit, then run for it and seize someone's hem in token of asking for protection.

'You are a Syrian,' he told me, pronouncing all his words with a heavy German accent.

I asked him what I could do for him.

'I like to know who is here, and who is not here. I like to know that there are no spies about.'

'Listen, brother Suleiman,' I said, overcome with indignation, 'you have no means of telling who is a spy and who is not, even in a place like this. There is no town, no huddle of huts, in the whole East which does not feel that there are spies about. Nobody ever bothers to wonder what they would be spying on. A spy in Nefta, ha!'

Suleiman laughed. 'All right. But this is the way one gets, in all this loneliness. I have made the Sahara my home, and I am bound to suffer from her sicknesses, am I not?'

'If you want to talk, talk,' I said.

'I am a Saharan, now. I was for years in Tripolitania, and I have been accepted as a dependent by the Beni Seif tribe. They took care of me when I was wounded and almost dying. I have been in business in this area for several years.'

I asked him what kind of business. Safe-conduct for caravans, he said; the buying and selling of dates; bringing to Nefta things 'that people could not officially get'.

'I cannot leave,' he said 'because my experience could not be used elsewhere.'

'Do you deal in arms?'

'Yes, who does not? Are you interested in automatic weapons?'

'No, I am a traveller, and that is all.'

At that moment Hamid came past, looking for me. He

headed for the table, saw the stranger, seemed to decide that he was safe, and sat down.

'People and safety. The Sheikh of the Azimiyya wants to see you, and sends his salutations. I am tired and have drunk too much mint tea.'

'I am Suleiman Ranjour, client of the Tribe of Seif,' said the Captain.

'May you be blessed,' said Hamid, 'and may your sheep and your goats prosper, and may your family flourish.' He looked at the Mauser, which Ranjour was again playing with. 'O my Lord and repository of Lordliness,' he continued prudently.

Suleiman got up. 'My rallying-cry is *Ya Ghanim* – O Success' he said, 'if you want to call me or send me a message.' It also means 'O Looter' said Hamid, somewhat fortified by this time by his rest. The German laughed and returned to his tribal friend, who was now telling the huge carved beads of a rosary which he carried suspended about his neck.

As we left the café, life seemed to take on a brisker tone. I decided that things seemed happier now because we had had a human contact, because the Sheikh would see us. We were again on the threshold of an event, instead of at the end of one.

'I feel that I understand the air of this oasis a little better now,' I said to Hamid.

'When you meet the Sheikh you will feel it still more strongly. So far you have not been in the Sahara, nor out of it,' he replied in what I was accustomed to regard as his enigmatic voice.

Surrounded by a number of small, dumpy domes, as much of Africa as Arabia, the zawiya of the Sheikh was sheltered by a row of very respectably sized trees, and there was an artesian well in the courtyard, where visiting dervishes refreshed themselves. Some wore little more than two jute sacks stitched together. Other looked for all the world like Oxford dons, with their hoods and dark sleeved robes, from which western academic garb is said to be ultimately derived. Yet others carried over their shoulders the *khirqa*, the patchwork robe of their first investiture.

Of the sixty or so present around the well, one had laid aside during his ablutions a red-pink, gold-embroidered ceremonial robe of an Emir of the Naqshbandi Order. These are the silent dervishes, one of the most widespread Orders, whose observances are secret and whose powers are supposed to be enormous. He was wearing felt boots, and had a Mongolian cast of feature. It was not impossible that he had walked from Central Asia to 'make the Visit' to the shrine which we were about to enter.

Beyond the courtyard a low doorway of Moorish horseshoe shape gave entrance to the Hall of Assembly, which served as school, gymnasium and prayer-hall for the community. Here the Sheikh sat, a small, neat figure in white turban and hooded robe, in the midst of his court. The mystics present sat in a circle with wide gaps in it, each on his small rug, all looking attentively towards their teacher. As we entered the room, he rose in token of great welcome. I gave the signal which is taught to each Sufi by his preceptor, indicating that I had come to learn from Sheikh Arif of Nefta, and we sat with crossed legs on the carpeted floor.

Then the story which formed part of that day's teaching was resumed. It was intended to illustrate that, whereas all human beings might want to perform good actions, it was often impossible to foresee whether an action carried out in good faith would produce a good result. What was the way out of this dilemma? Through the *baraka* (spiritual force) of the Order, said the Sheikh, its members acquired a power known as *yakina,* which was an inner certainty that this or that action was for the real and ultimate good of mankind. The story was long, but it pointed the moral well enough.

Then came a pause for an incense-burner to be brought in by a novice, and we all in turn passed our hands over the smoke which poured from it. When mint tea was brought, the Sheikh turned to me, and asked me my mission. I told him that I was studying the teachings of the Sufis, and comparing what I heard, in each centre of instruction, with a view to understanding exactly what this system was. He explained to me many things which I had already been told about the cult in Central Asia: and a good many more about their philosophy of action.

Sufism, he maintained, was the source of religion. All the religious teachers had been Sufis. 'Sufism is the milk, and religion is the butter, after it has been churned. You cannot taste the milk for the butter. We drink the milk.'

He was well read, in French as well as in Arabic and Persian, and had something to say about the relationship of his system with others. He did not believe that Sufism was an Islamic revolt against the austerity of the Prophet's creed, nor that it owed anything to India, to Buddhism or to neo-platonism.

'The superficial resemblances seized by scholars on the outside to account for our ways are not due to a cause-and-effect relationship,' he told me; 'rather are they due to the fact that the basis of our activity is to be found in all human minds. We alone, however, have systematised it, and can produce its full effect upon the human being. The goal is to make the Perfected Man.'

After a long conversation on these lines, the Sheikh told me that I was to be allowed to be present ('although you are of low rank in the Way') at one of the religious exercises – the *Dhikr* – of the dervishes. This was the first real *Dhikr* which I had attended; for private exercises of this kind are not open to strangers. I was grateful for the opportunity.

The *Dhikr*, it was explained to me, is a dance: or, more properly, a performance of a series of exercises in unison. The objective is to produce a state of ritual ecstasy and to accelerate the contact of the Sufi's mind with the world-mind of which he considers himself to be a part. In view of the recent widespread interest in ecstatic states in the West, in which drugs like Mescalin, LSD (lysergic acid) and hallucinogenic toadstools were used, I felt that I might learn something that would be of abiding interest.

All dervishes, and not only the followers of Maulana Rumi (as most Orientalists erroneously believe) perform a dance. And a dance is defined as bodily movements linked to a thought and a sound or a series of sounds. The movements develop the body, the thought focuses the mind, and the sound fuses the two and orientates them towards a consciousness of divine contact which is called '*hal*' and means 'state or condition': the state or condition of being in ecstasy.

Armed with this information, I took my place in the double circle which was being formed in the centre of the hall. The dervishes stood while the Sheikh intoned the opening part of this and every similar ceremony: the calling down of the blessing upon the congregation, and from the congregation upon the Masters of the 'past, present and future'. Outside the circles stood the Sheikh, a drummer and a flute player, together with two 'callers': the men who called the rhythm of the dance.

The drum began to beat, and the callers started to sing a high-pitched, flamenco-like tune, eerie and penetrating. Slowly the concentric circles began to revolve, each in the opposite direction, myself included, edging along, concentrating upon the sound. Then the Sheikh called out 'Ya Haadi!' – 'O Guide' (one of the ninety-nine names of Allah) and the participants started to repeat this word, as they concentrated upon it, first slowly, then faster and faster. Their movements matched the repetition. I noticed that the eyes of some of the dervishes took on a faraway look, and they started to move jerkily, as if they were puppets.

The circles moved faster and faster, until I (moving in the outer circle) saw only a whirl of robes, and lost count of time. Now and then, with a grunt, or a sharp cry, one of the dervishes would drop out of the circle, and would be led away by an assistant, to lie on the ground in what seemed to be an hypnotic state. I began to be affected, and found that although I was not dizzy, my mind was functioning in a very strange and unfamiliar way. The sensation is difficult to describe, and is probably a complex one. One feeling was that of a lightening: as if I had no anxieties, no problems. Another was that I was a part of this moving circle, and that my individuality was gone, was delightfully merged in something larger.

Eventually, as the movements continued, I had the sensation that I must somehow tear myself away. And, oddly enough, as soon as the thought occurred to me, I found it easy to leave the group. As I stepped from the circle, I was taken by the elbow by the Sheikh, who looked at me closely, smiling.

It was only when I started to talk to him that I realised that it was impossible: the dervishes were producing such a penetrating buzz of sound that it would have been impossible to hear anything else. I looked at my watch. Two hours had passed in what seemed but a few minutes.

I went out into the courtyard, to assess my feelings. Something *had* happened. In the first place, the moon seemed immensely bright, and the little glowing lamps seemed surrounded by a whole spectrum of colours. My mind was working by a system of associations of some kind: because as soon as I thought of a thing, it was almost as if one thought bore another, until my mind lighted upon a logical consequence. An example may make this clearer. The lamps reminded me of a stained-glass window; and the window of an argument I had had with a friend some months before, near a church. This, in turn, focused my attention upon this friend, and then, like a flash, I saw him in my mind shaking hands with a red-bearded man. Then the whole thing faded. This sort of experience remained with me for about a month, during which time I could reproduce it by thinking of the lamps.

When, later, I went to Paris and met this friend, I found that he had gone into partnership with a red-bearded man. This experience closely paralleled, therefore, one experienced a few years ago during a ritual by Mr. Wasson, the American authority on Mexican mushrooms. In his case there was a vision of his son in unfamiliar circumstances, which turned out to be correct.

The ritual continued, and the Sheikh took me into his private room, where we sat on cushions and talked about the meaning of the *Dhikr*.

'We are widely accused of magic,' he said, 'and, since magic has the sanction of Islam inasmuch as the Prophet said that it exists, I do not dispute it. But we are working in a different medium. Without the "strange experience" we cannot become perfected. Take this analogy: all experience in the world is, in in fact, strange. When it becomes habit or commonplace, one does not regard it as experience. But it is essential, is it not, to the learning process?'

'I realise that you are not trying to impress me,' I said to Sheikh Arif, 'but I have a largely Western approach to such things as those which we have seen tonight. Would you allow me to test some of your dervishes to establish whether they are in any sort of an hypnotic state familiar to Westerners?'

'Gladly,' he said, 'though that would not invalidate anything, from our point of view; because what you call hypnosis is merely the beginning of something; the visible part of something that remains invisible to you.'

We returned to the meeting-hall, to find that several of the Sufis were still circling around. In order to be sure that I would be in a more objective frame of mind, I decided that I should postpone the test until another day. Most obligingly, the Sheikh told me to come when I liked. Collecting Hamid from the kitchens, where he was sampling the steaming pots of that night's rations, I went to my quarters to write notes.

The following morning the Sheikh sent word that he would be pleased to see us as soon as we liked. Hamid was not too sanguine about the success of an examination of dervishes in a state of 'hal', but came along to the assembly-room. Here we found the Sheikh eating a hearty breakfast from a bowl of meat and gravy. Pleading an indisposition, I refused the food, just in case it might have some hallucinogenic ingredient. Dervishes came in and out, shaking hands and saying 'Ishq' (Love) and then kissing their own hands. The Sheikh explained to them what we wanted, and though some did not seem to approve, we were left with eleven who might be termed the volunteers.

After a night's sleep, the Sheikh seemed completely won over to my idea, and rather peremptorily called the musicians and started the dance. I held my watch in my hand, timing the music and waiting for the first to pass into an ecstatic state. The first thing that I noticed was that the proceeding did not seem to affect those who did not take part in the dance. The music and rhythm seemed to be the same as on the previous night.

After six minutes the first dervish – a man of about forty – swayed and was led from the group. As soon as he sat down he seemed to lose consciousness. When prodded, he showed no sign of life and he was breathing very shallowly. I opened his eyelid, but the eyeball was not turned up. The pupils were not dilated or contracted, neither did they react to light when I lit my cigarette lighter.

Out of the eleven participants, nine were in a state of *'hal'* after two hours. Unlike normally hypnotised people, they did not respond to words spoken to them; neither did they show the almost complete immobility which is one of the characteristics of the hypnotised person. Although anaesthesia of the nerves is normally produced only by suggestion to that effect, they did not seem to feel pinpricks or tickling applied without any suggestions. This did not seem to be a familiar form of hypnosis. Ordinary hypnosis normally passes into sleep. But these volunteers woke up direct into wakefulness without sleep supervening. What was more, there was no amnesia, and throughout they had been aware of what had been said and done to them; although in at least some cases (had this been normal hypnosis) partial amnesia could have been expected at this depth of hypnosis.

The next part of my test was to attempt to induce normal hypnosis. Only three out of the eleven passed into the lightest form of conventional hypnosis, which was the proportion which would be expected in a random sample of this size. None showed any evidence that they were conditioned: that is to say, that they were accustomed to passing into hypnosis of any kind, let alone a deep-trance state.

All this added up to the strong possibility that the trance into which these people threw themselves was not of a kind familiar to the West. In all cases they reported transcendental experiences during the trance : and two of them even purported to have read my thoughts. They claimed that they knew, when in trance, as to what I was going to try next, as a test.

None of this material, of course, is scientifically conclusive. What could be of paramount importance might be that the drumming and intonations contained a signal to which the subjects had been conditioned. I resolved to make tape-recordings of some future session, and replay them at intervals with similar volunteers, to see whether a later part of the proceedings would produce the trance more quickly when played back. This, however, would have to wait until I was better equipped.

The rest of my stay at the Zawiya was passed in taking notes of the methods of teaching and the theories which the Sufis passed on. In day-by-day instruction, two sessions were held. One was for younger initiates, who were passing through a thousand-and-one-days' novitiate. The other meeting was that to which 'Seekers' – adepts – were admitted. The disciples had to carry out memorising and meditative exercises, developing powers of concentration and reflection. The others, it seemed, were keeping up a sort of training of which thought and work, as well as exercises like the *Dhikr,* all formed a part.

After a few days, the air of mystery and strangeness which I had felt was replaced by a sensation that, however unfamiliar these practices might seem to the outsider, their devotees did not regard them as supernatural as we might use the term. As Sheikh Arif once said: 'We are doing something which is natural, which is the result of research and practice into the future development of mankind; we are producing a *new* man.

And we do it for no material gain.' This, then, is their attitude.

When we returned to civilisation, and Hamid and I took leave of one another amid the streamlined motor-cars and fashionable clothes of Tunis, we knew that our deliberately anachronistic caravan trip to the sands of the Sahara had been well worth while. We had, in a sense, re-entered the Middle Ages; whatever the truth of the Sufi belief that the dervishes were creating a new man. And I, for one, was determined to penetrate again into that world-within-a-world which is the land of the Sufis.

CHAPTER FOUR

Istanbul

If, in characteristic Arabian Nights manner, I had been able to gain entry to Mecca through a letter from an Oriental, I had a very different experience in Turkey. For Turkey has been westernised, and Western things work there.

As soon as I reached Istanbul, I went from Mosque to Mosque seeking dervish contacts. I went to places where I thought such illegal remnants might linger, such as the University theology faculty, the school of arts and crafts, the cultural museums. Religious piety there was plenty, but signs of the dervishes – none.

Istanbul, though impressive and still evocative of an imperial past, is hot and dusty in the Summer, and I could only keep going through its endless streets by frequent stops for coffee. At one teashop I got into conversation with the proprietor, because he had a Sufic calligraphic emblem over his samovar. We had to speak German, because that was the only foreign language he knew.

I started by asking the usual questions, saying that I was a British student of Islamics, on holiday, and that I wanted to find a dervish.

'There are none left. The last ones were hanged.'

'But there must be *some* who have escaped or were not caught.'

'There are none.'

'But there must be some.'

'There may be some.'

'Where would a person look for them?'

'He would have to have time.'

'But I have no time.'

'If you have no time, you have no chance.'

'Where would one look?'

'Have you a written?'

A 'written' can mean anything. In this kind of context, however, it tends to mean 'some documentary evidence of your probity or importance.'

I showed him my dervish belt. He looked at it with great interest and handed it back to me.

I did not have a 'written'.

I went back to my coffee, gloomily. In Morocco, Sidi el-Hajj had advised me to travel to Turkey, had said that I would be able to study Sufis there without any of the complications attendant upon the cult's being dressed in mediaeval clothes in Arab lands, or even Central Asia. I had obtained an introduction to Dr. Karabek Murat, through the Sage's good offices. But Murat was away for the Summer, or so they told me at his villa at Bebek. And this in spite of the fact that Bebek itself was a Summer resort on the Bosphorus.

Hence my wandering through the streets of Istanbul all that dusty day.

This chasing of dervishes seemed to have its own problems – different in each one of the countries which I visited. It was true that I was recording information that did not seem to exist in any permanent form in the West, but the whole effort at times did seem more like a spy-story than anything else. Secret assignations, signals, identifications, people not at home. . . .

So I decided to follow up the unsolved absence of Dr Murat and return to Bebek. When the creaky old municipal omnibus eventually deposited me before the villa again, I marched up to the door without any fixed plan as to what I would say if I was again met by the crone who spoke only a few words of French, and a great deal of Turkish.

I rang the bell below the engraved plate *Doctor-Operator Karabek MURAT,* as the sun was setting. A middle-aged man answered the door. I said, in English, 'I have come to see Dr Murat, *eren*'. The last word means 'dervish', or, more literally, 'One who has attained'.

'I am Murat,' said the doctor, and threw the door open for me to enter. When I had introduced myself, he said, 'You would not have come back if you had been an agent-provocateur, but you don't transmit me any *barakat.*'

He was dressed in a shirt and trousers, and slipped on a sports coat as he said, 'Let us drive into Town, and have a bite before we take you to a meeting.'

We went outside, called a cab, and dined by the sea at the modern side of the city, the Taksim area.

During the meal I asked Murat about the meaning of the Koran. I knew that it had been passed on by Mohammed, piecemeal, taken down on pieces of skin, leather and bones, collected into one authoritative version and preserved thus for nearly thirteen hundred years. I knew, too, that many people committed the whole volume (it is about the same length as the New Testament) to heart, and that there were various specialised methods of reciting it. The Koran is regarded with the same awe today as when it was first received, because nobody has been able to compose anything in this rhythm (it is all rhymed) with anything like the strange effect which it has upon its hearers.

Legends about the Koran persist. People carry it, or certain passages from it, as talismans. It is recited at all important events of life, such as birth, marriage or death. The title *Hafiz* ('protector') of the Koran, given to those who have it all by memory, is highly prized.

But what *is* the Koran? According to Islamic belief it is the very word of God, transmitted by the Angel Gabriel to Mohammed. It is a terrestrial copy of something which exists in Heaven inscribed in something called the 'Preserved Tablet'. What is the Koran to the Sufis?

Murat at first evaded the question. Then he suddenly said: 'You have asked about the Merciful Koran. You have asked me, unmindful of the fact that Sufism depends upon time and place, *Zaman wa Makan,* for its ability to transmit real knowledge. Now I will tell you *something* about it.

'The Koran is the product of a greater Being than man can normally perceive. It has been sent down into this sphere and as a result that part which is perceptible to men of this sphere will mean what it can to them. That part which is perceptible to the greater beings will be perceptible to them. Take an example: A man who cannot read or write sees a book. For all he knows it is a Koran. He may not know about the Koran. In these cases it is unlikely to be of use to him, unless he has special perceptions which render the knowledge of literacy redundant. A man who can read and write Arabic badly will not be able to understand as much as a man who knows it perfectly. An academic will be able to perceive it only academically, with a portion of emotionalism which is engendered in him by training.

'But the Koran was sent down and entrusted to the breasts of men for a purpose. This purpose was not only that it should help to form a community believing what it said literally. The Koran itself says this, where it is repeated that allegories are used. What is the use of an allegory? Why, simply to take a mind into a realm where it can no longer think in the pedestrian way that scholars think. No, for the man who has to be civilised and prepared for another stage the Koran must be adhered to as literal truth. But for those who understand more, the higher developmental secrets will be available.'

I asked him for an example. He told me that any words in the Koran could be taken to illustrate this fact to an intelligent man, though more than intelligence was needed to get into contact with the higher meaning. 'Take the very first words of the Koran: "In the Name of Allah, the Beneficent, the Merciful." What is this name? *Allah* means "That worthy of worship." What is worship? What is beneficent? What is Merciful? The lowest level of man has only the conceptions which he understands by these words. "Beneficent" to him means something or someone who does him good. What kind of good? Good that he considers to be good? And so on. This illustrates that man reads words without knowing what they mean *because the meaning of the words alters in accordance with the experiences of the people using them.*'

He continued, 'There are vital secrets in the Koran. All history, all experience, all the pattern of creation are there. But each man or woman will be able to know just as much as he is capable of understanding of these, and the same is the case with the first chapter and the Moslem Prayer, as it is with the original prayers of Christianity, Judaism and other faiths, which have now been so edited by the ignorant that they are useless as sources of secret teaching.'

And he would say no more.

Was it possible, I asked myself, that a form of ancient knowledge of any importance to the human race still lingered in the under-developed and at times unattractive East? I brought up this matter with Murat.

He smiled, 'Your difficulty is that you find it hard to believe that a people possessed of anything of value could be so materially backward. Or that anything still remains secret in this world, when mass-communications are used to reproduce and spew forth knowledge in every form. But you do not realise that what you call this "ancient knowledge" may be of a kind which cannot yet be given to the world.'

'How can there be a time to give something to the world, and a time to withhold it?'

'If you give chemicals to a child he will destroy himself. When he is a man, he will use them constructively, perhaps in some industry.'

I said that I did not feel that he could patronise me like that without some evidence.

'It is not for me to give you evidence of anything. If a child says to you, "Give me evidence of the dangers of the chemicals you are said to possess," you are not obliged to do so.'

In the cool of the evening the sea lapped gently a few feet below us, the moonlight reflected from a million wavelets each like a facet of some dark and yet living jewel. Dr Murat raised his arm, pointing across the Golden Horn. 'There seems to be a myriad of moons,' he said, 'yet in reality there is only one. Humanity sees things like that; seeking diversity where there is really unity. Science, useful though it may be, is teaching more and more of us the false truth that everything, yes everything, is infinitely divisible.'

I recognised the analogy, for it was almost a direct quotation from the ancient Sufi teaching which I was travelling the world to study, and whose quest had brought me to Istanbul, most Western of the Eastern lands.

Twenty years ago, perhaps less, the voicing of such sentiments as these in modern, progressive Turkey would have been considered worse than merely bad taste. In the first flush of republicanism and Kemalist fervour, everything except nationalism had been thrown away. Allah had been dethroned, and the days of the Sublime Porte, the Sultan-Caliph, the harem and the dervish had gone for ever.

I had only been in Turkey for eight hours, and I wondered how typical Dr Murat was. He laughed, as if reading my thought. 'There is a settling down after a storm, you know.

Come, my friend, it is Thursday night, and we have a meeting to attend.'

Murat belonged to the philosophical school of the Naqsh-bandis, founded by a sage of Bokhara, and formerly one of the most important religious orders in the Turkish Empire. The Order had been dissolved in the nineteen-twenties under Kemal, because it was said to be associated with the mediaeval thinking of the clerics and a support of the Ottoman régime.

But if the Latin alphabet and European clothes had come to Turkey, there were some things which it was more difficult to eradicate. We took a vehicle marked *Taksi* (there is no X in Turkish) – not to some dark monastery, but to a towering new block of flats in the new part of the city.

Murat rang a bell, and we were shown by a manservant into a large, modern-furnished room, where about thirty people were chatting and drinking tiny cups of bitter coffee. For all the world we might have been at a smart cocktail party anywhere in the West: except that no alcohol was being served. Murat introduced me to various guests. One was an Army officer, another a civil servant, a third a merchant; all in their middle thirties. Men and women were about evenly represented.

I asked the officer how it was that Sufism still survived in this progressive country, and whether he thought that a way of life which was described almost unanimously in reference books as a product of the Middle Ages could survive. He laughed. 'I do not know anything at all about the Middle Ages,' he said, 'but I do know that without this *Tarika* (Right Way) we would never had survived in Korea. Instead of Thursday-night meetings we had daily ones among the men. Together, lying in foxholes and waiting for hordes of yelling Chinese to attack, we exchanged stories of the perfectability of humanity, talked about the destiny of the human race, spoke of generosity, love and high-mindedness. This is the Sufi way as I see it.' I had heard that the Army restored Moslem chaplains for the purposes of the Korean war. Which did he think was the most potent factor in binding the men together: patriotism, Islam or Sufism?

'All are essential. Sufism is practical. You see, it does not only preach an ideal, it gives a way in which this ideal can be given expression in our lives.'

I knew from my wanderings among Sufi communities elsewhere that the 'intuitive answer' played a large part in the system. So I asked the soldier:

'Can you give me an intuitive answer to the question. "What is Sufism?" ' This form of statement is thought by Sufis to be almost inspired, to come from the very depths of the being, and to be in a sense authoritative and to hold true for the specific time and place in which it is given.

He closed his eyes for a moment. 'Yes, Sufism is humanity, the link between the past, the present and the future. It is understood and expressed through love, and its instrument is generosity of spirit. It reveals itself in the lives of all good people, and conceals itself from those who seek to analyse it. Ultimately it will prevail throughout humanity, because it is there, inside all of us, waiting to be used. Love and generosity imply many other things, like loyalty, high-mindedness and service.'

As we were talking, the chatter around us died away, and I noticed that everyone was looking towards an alcove through which a tall, smiling woman had entered the room. A high, stirring note sounded on a reed-flute held by a youth who was sitting beside the door; a haunting melody not unlike bagpipe-music, which spoke of deep emotion and dignity. 'This is the Friend – a teacher' whispered my companion.

While a semicircle of chairs was being arranged facing the place where the Friend would sit to address us, I was able to study her more closely as she spoke to Murat. She must have been about twenty-eight, with the remarkably white skin and black hair which characterises many Turkish beauties. She was dressed in a green suit of Western style, and wore a silver ring with an almond-shaped turquoise set into it. We all sat down, and the lady started to speak, somewhat to my surprise, in English.

'We have a guest tonight, and I will talk in his language. Here is a parable from the *Mathnawi* of the great master Rumi, about the value of mutual concentration. In the original Persian, of course, the story is versified and the impact of it is greater. But it also has its teaching side, which is reserved for the assemblies of the Sufis, and not written down.

'There was a sage, the wisest man of his age, called Lukman, who went one day to see David the king, father of Solomon. David was sitting among a pile of metallic rings, and he was making one fit into the next. Lukman was intensely curious, and at first thought that he would ask what manner of art this was. But, being wise though uninstructed in intuition, he decided that he would wait until he could see what would be the product of this strange activity. Patience, he told himself, was the key to inner understanding. Paradoxically, patience is faster than haste: for through haste nothing of the interior mind is understood. The secret, as we know, shields itself equally against stupidity and hurry.

'Presently, therefore, as the rings were added to one another, a coat of fine mail emerged: for David was the first man to devise this garment. Turning to Lukman, David said: "This will protect one from the fight" and he donned it.

'Now these metallic rings are called *Halka,* circles; and the name which we give to our assemblies is also *halka,* and thus the master Rumi has taught the value of the meetings which we hold. They preserve and sharpen our inner faculties, so that our outer ways may be perfected.'

I had read this story of Rumi's, both in Persian and in many translations, but this interpretation had never been offered to me before; although it is a fair example of the preaching methods within the Sufi *halka.*

The Friend raised her arms, and all present followed suit. This was the moment of the calling down of the *baraka* (spiritual power) into the assembly; believed by all Sufis to confer abilities which appear supernatural to the outside world.

When this and other observances were over, I was able to speak to the lady. Like the others, she had a Sufi name – Arifa, the Wise. This Westernised atmosphere, I realised, was ideal in one respect. I could now ask questions about the supernaturalism of Sufism; questions which were difficult to put in the traditional surroundings of the monasteries that I had visited in the East. Take it how you will, it was evident that she knew what I was about to say. I do not rule out coincidence or keen observation – or merely putting two and two together.

'I hear from Murat,' she said, her eyes twinkling, 'that you are one of us, and that you have come far to see us. A very great deal of present-day Sufist belief in Turkey is based upon the fact that we have verified what are often called the "miracles" of the ancients. But we do not rely upon these signs, as we consider them inferior to intuition – right thinking. A person who is attracted to a thing because of its sensation value is probably not ready for enlightenment.'

I decided to get straight to the point. 'Sheikh Abdul Qadir of Gilan,' I said, 'according to witnesses, once threw his slippers into the air during a Sufi meeting. Three days later a caravan arrived at his residence, and its members claimed that on that very day a pair of slippers, which they had with them, struck two bandits who were at that very moment robbing them, and this happening was so supernatural that it put the robbers to flight. Did this actually happen, or is the interpretation figurative, or is the whole story a fabrication?'

Arifa threw back her head and laughed. 'It is for people like you that the rope-trick is performed. The answer is really none of these things. But, to use your terms, the nearest we can get is to say that this thing could easily have happened. How it happened, and why, is something that you understand through experience. And experience does not mean thinking out and explaining in words; but having these things happen to you. If you only knew it, such things are happening all the time to you. What you take as coincidence, or accident, very often is action : action taking place on a plane which is invisible to you. This does not mean that the illuminated Sufi sees and knows all : he or she only knows as much as is necessary for the time and the place.'

The following day, Arifa and Murat took me to the old part of the city, among the honeycombing streets of ancient Istanbul, to visit Fikri Bey, an ancient of the Order who was much more like the Sufi Sheikhs of Arab lands, though he, too, wore Western clothes.

Fikri may have been ninety – but he did not know his age. He spoke Arabic and Persian as well as Turkish, and had been in Ottoman government service, and had been initiated into three of the four main Sufi orders. Some years before World War II, he told me, he had lived in one of the Bokhara Sufi centres, and he had many of the sayings of the teachers by heart. We spoke of the past and the future of Sufism, and whether it would be of any interest to the West. I told him that modern people took little on trust, were not prepared (on the whole) to repose confidence in people who were supposed to be able to guide their inner development, without concrete evidence. One might say that they lacked faith. He interrupted with a snort, his wrinkled face upturned, steel-grey eyes narrowed.

'There has always been a lack of faith: this is no new problem. Religion has civilised people more than you think. At one time a teacher would be ignored or hanged. Today he will get a hearing. As to faith in the West, I know little about it. But remember, when you go to a tailor to have a suit made, you use intelligence and logic to get you to the tailor's door. After you have chosen the cloth and given your order, you abandon all to the tailor. This is faith. I doubt whether mechanisation has changed the situation for you in the West, either. What you need is to realise that you use faith every day. Where the clerics go wrong is to harangue people, saying that they have none. Rather should they point out what faith is, where it is to be seen in man; and encourage people to develop it. The land has to be tilled before the seed can sprout. We shall till the soil, and then the rain will fall. From the half-dozen seeds which have been planted, one or two will come to fruition. We will not reap, because we shall be overcome by devastation for a hundred years. But this man, though he does not know, will prepare the ground.'

Sufi tradition has it that 'intermediaries' often prepare the ground for the Sufi message. The strange thing about this doctrine is that the 'intermediary' is someone who is temporarily or permanently endowed with a minimum of *baraka* (power): and such a man or woman is largely unconscious of what he is actually destined to do. I was to find this theory in full development in India, where cults like the blend of Sufism and Yoga were flourishing.

Across Anatolia, where the Turk still feels and thinks in very much the same way as have his forebears through the centuries, I journeyed to the tomb of the mystic Jalaludin Rumi at Konia in Asiatic Turkey. The tomb is very much like those of other Sufi teachers, with the teacher's turban set above an embroidered cloth which covers the catafalque. Everywhere is seen the inscription, still in Arabic letters, which is the slogan of the Mevlevi Order: '*Yaa hadrat Maulana* – O Presence, Our Master!'

Sufis of every class of society perform the 'visit' to the tomb, and meditate here upon the unity of humanity and the unity of spiritual things taught by the founder of the dancing dervishes.

He was born in Balkh, Afghanistan, in 1207 A.D., and was buried in Konia where he taught for most of his life, at the age of sixty-six. Such was his repute and his insistence upon brotherhood that members of five faiths followed his bier. His teachings took the form of fables and stories, carrying out mystical exercises, and setting his disciples tasks which were to be carried out in everyday life. Some of these involved excelling in their chosen career. He is noted for two specific ideas: the first that mankind is the product of evolution; and the second that the human soul is cut off from 'the parent stem'. It is, according to Rumi, essential for humanity to find its way back, through labour and self-development, to that harmony with creation whose loss is the cause of unhappiness. The method is love.

Rumi wrote in Persian, and hence is regarded by the people of Iran as one of their national poets. Certain it is that his work is some of the most sublime literature ever known. The Afghans claim him, because of his birthplace being Balkh – Bactria – and the Turks revere him because he taught on their soil. He was not influenced by the poetry of Omar Khayyam, who belonged to the same philosophical school; but many of the ideas of the Sufis are shared by these two master-poets.

Omar's teaching method was to draw attention to the limitations of what one generally regards as the security of life, and also to advocate that everyone should at some time endure opprobrium, in order to 'refine' himself. Further, he spoke of the rewards which are available in this world for those who follow the Sufi way. Rumi, for his part, places great emphasis upon the fact that few can see the true reality of situations. Further, he insists, the intellectual and scholastic methods, though immensely valuable, are not the all-in-all. He believes that real knowledge is the product of intuition, not of formal learning, which is a separate discipline.

A newspaper editor whom I met in Ankara referred to present-day problems by way of a story of Rumi's, to the effect that things may in reality not be what they seem to you or me. This is the tale: a well-meaning old woman found an eagle perched on her window-sill. It looked to her rather strange to be a bird; for she had never seen one like it before. So she took pity on it. First she snipped off its crest, then she cut its crook-beak straight; finally she clipped its (to her) over-sized wings: and then she set it free, saying, 'Now you look more like a bird'. The maimed bird now looked like a pigeon. This is what scholastics do to wisdom.

Thus do Sufi teachings, perhaps more than any other, course through the life of Turkey today, on many different levels. In the villages the ritual observances take the form of private meetings at which the sacred dance and song are performed. In more sophisticated circles, books refer surprisingly often to the message of the Sufis as being interpretable in terms of human social evolution. I was delighted when, in a small village perched on a hillside, I was able to talk to a middle-aged man who had spent several years in America; part of the time as one of the near-legendary New York taxi-drivers. He took me into his tiny wooden house, where we sat, enjoying the vista over the hills beneath a twisting vine, and he talked about the nature of religion as he understood it. He chose a chapter from – none other than Rumi.

'You ask me,' he said, 'what we think here of the differences in religion, in politics, in ways of life. How, in fact, could all the people of the world find something in common, and live in harmony. I am a Turk. As such, I have had to fight, and fight I will again, at any moment, because this may be expected of me. But we have a tradition about this question, which I will tell you:

An elephant had been brought from a far country, and it was being kept in a dark stable. Some people entered, and as they could not see, they started to feel their way. The first man felt the ears, and thought that they were fans. The second felt the legs, and concluded that they were pillars. The third, touching the trunk, felt sure that this must be a snake. They had no lantern with them, otherwise there would have been no discord of opinion. Opinion, you see, is based upon fragmentary, not total, experience.'

This wonderful analogy which shows how people judge things through their own subjectivity, and which hints at the possibility of a 'lantern' is straight from the pages of the master Rumi. Was the 'lantern' a man, a way of looking at things, a book, a stage of society? 'I think,' said my new friend, 'that it is there whenever people come together, and desire to be together.'

In Ankara, the modern capital city built by Mustafa Kemal on the site of an ancient settlement dating back many milennia, I was lucky enough to learn of the forthcoming gathering of dervishes to be held in the south. My Sufi friends there arranged for me to share expenses with one of the delegates. Since he is a highly-placed civil servant I shall call my travelling companion Rashad. Together we drove across Anatolia, through Eskishehr to Izmir, the former Smyrna, on the Aegean Sea.

Wherever we stopped, people were wonderfully hospitable. In the countryside many women were still veiled, and people continued to use the Arabic alphabet instead of the officially-sponsored Latin one. Many a time we spent hours in wayside *Chaihanes* (teahouses) where the proprietor's son or daughter would be brought forward, sometimes a little triumphantly, I thought, to show me how they could trace the Arabic alphabet. Wherever we went fruit and flowers, some token of our passing, was pressed upon us.

Izmir is a flourishing city, modernised, so I was told, out of all recognition since the Revolution of forty years before. Its climate is excellent and although the ancient Grand Bazaar sold mostly reproductions of the ancient wares, it was still intriguing and Oriental.

The conference of mystics was held in a private house in the suburb of Karatas. Some fifty delegates, each representing a 'province' (*Vilayat*) had assembled from as far afield as Ethiopia, the Persian Caspian and Burma. Turkey, Afghanistan, India and Pakistan were among the countries represented.

Because of Turkey's sensitivity towards the Sufis, all the 'delegates' had come as tourists, many of them overland by way of Beirut. They were parcelled out as guests in various hotels or staying in the houses of sympathisers. Sometimes local representatives were there instead of delegates from the various countries. The sheikh of the Egyptian Qadiri Order, for instance, was represented by his Caliph, a bookseller from Istanbul.

This was, I was told, the first world conference of Sufis in this form which had been held for a thousand years or more. Two types were represented. First, there was the conventional kind, somewhat resembling the monks of medieval Christendom, who concentrated upon religious formulae and practices derived from the Moslem scriptures. Secondly, there were the 'silent dervishes', those who believed that the 'higher man' (*rajal aali*) could communicate with the absolute without words or rituals.

Both parties had come to Turkey primarily to collect and 'store' the accumulated spiritual force which they all believed resided in certain centres, deposited there by the saints and teachers who had lived, taught and often died there.

In many ways Sufism as understood by these people resembled a sort of invisible science. Although time and space were of little account to them, several insisted that by coming to Turkey they were able to 'contact the baraka' of Rumi, or the Shrine of Ayyoub near Istanbul, or Telli Baba on the Bosphorus, and many others. When they spoke, it was almost as if one was hearing about technicians or scientists discussing an unknown force or wave, with which they could communicate.

Only the Pakistanis spoke of formal organisation, and about the formation, which had recently taken place, of an Assembly of Mystics in Pakistan, to which President Ayub Khan belonged, and which consisted, it seemed, of the heads of all the Sufi teaching schools in that country. But these obviously belonged to the 'overt' side of Sufism, and they tended to regard Sufism as a religious quest, to be carried out entirely through the doctrines of Islam.

There was no doubt that something which cannot be easily accounted for in normal terms, suffused the assembly at Karatas. I gained the impression that all these people had been called together for a purpose which was only vaguely perceptible in their talk and their exchanging of reminiscences.

The representative of the Rector of Deobund University, the dervish-cum-Islamic institution in North India, invited me to Delhi. I decided to go there, for I had not been in that country before, and in any case I wanted to return to Pakistan and Afghanistan later in the year. Deobund is one of the most revered foundations in the Moslem world, and had never been known to admit within its walls other than the most orthodox followers of the faith. It is recognised as a teaching institution of high importance by even al-Azhar in Cairo, and there is a strong connexion between it and the Central Asians.

CHAPTER FIVE

A Group of Callandars

'We must stop here,' said Spin Dil, his enormous Pathan hand decisively drawing the handbrake. His head turned, and the impassive sniper's gaze stared me out until I was in no position to question the decision of one who was, after all, my employee.

The sun beat down with the warmth of a hot English summer day, and the white, dusty snake of the Indian road seemed to slumber in the vastness of Uttar Pradesh – what used to be called the United Provinces of British India.

A village, half-hidden by the incline, the banking of the highway, lay to our left, like half a million other Indian villages; quiet in the middle of the day, undeveloped to our Western eye, devoid of any picturesque charm, poverty-stricken for a surety.

Spin Dil the Khattak clansman, a warrior of the Khyber land whose name in Pushtu means white ('pure') heart was not a one for too much sentimentalising but he knew his duty. 'Over there,' he said, 'in the hollow, within half rifle-shot, is the Dargah of Pir Callandar. We go there.'

A little distance from the village was a low wall, and behind it the dome and chamber which mark the burial-places of Moslem mystics. It was not a pretentious place, but it did have its air of other-worldliness, and I scrambled after Spin Dil until we were at the well which lay before the entrance to the shrine. Over the low doorway was a stone on which we could just make out in the Perso-Arabic characters which are today being widely replaced by the Hindu Devanagri script, the message that this was the resting place of the *Pir-i-Bedar,* the Wakeful Sage. 'Pir' means, literally, 'ancient, old', but it can be used for quite young men, when they have reached the stage of teacher, and when they have disciples. It is equivalent to *Guru* in Hindi, and a certain type of Sheikh in Arabic. The Khattak, with his fair skin and grey eyes, his European suit combated only by a conical skullcap and wisp of turban, looked like a Westerner. He had worked for a diplomatic family in New Delhi, and like all Pathans, took eagerly to Western ways – up to a point. The build of the Pathan is more suited to double-breasted garb than is the more delicate Indian frame. He even wore his trousers fashionably tapered. He took a small coin out of his waistcoat pocket, weighed it a moment in his palm, then threw it like a cricketer over the dome. 'You can do that, too,' he looked down at me from his immense height, with a toothy grin, not in the least ashamed of his superstition. 'The Pir's influence will bring us what we need; he works in the invisible world.'

I threw a rupee over the dome, not quite knowing whether I should have wished or not. 'Well,' said Spin Dil, 'let us go.'

As we sped towards Meerut, my companion, who had early established himself as something more than a mere employee, told me about the strange community to which the saint had belonged. The meaning of their name – Callandar – is, like the word Sufi which is used for mystics in the Middle East, mysterious in origin. Some say that it was deliberately coined in order to avoid the associations which would attach to any real name. The nearest sounds to this one in local languages is Qaal, in Turkish, which means 'pure'; or *Kalaantar,* which in Persian refers to a chief of some sort. The Callandars themselves usually decline to discuss the matter.

It is difficult to tell a Callandar from a Fakir; partly because they sometimes refer to themselves as either, but mostly because they sometimes wander the countryside dressed in hardly anything at all, are revered and sometimes feared, and are reputed to have magical powers. This is one of the Orders of dervishes which has the most in common with Hindu Fakirs, with whom they are often on the best of terms. When we got to town I asked the frontier man to try to put me in touch with a Callandar who, as I understood it, were in short supply. 'One of the difficulties,' said Spin Dil, 'is that people who are on the surface perfectly normal may turn out to be callandars. On the other hand, when you do actually meet a callandar on the road, he may not talk to you, because he is an ordinary man on an extra-ordinary errand.' What exactly did he mean? Well, people sometimes took vows to become callandars for a time; or they might be under the orders of their superior to carry out a wandering spell, and they would then be concentrating upon whatever it was that they had to do. It looked as though I might have to wait a very long time for an interview with a callandar. But in the end I was luckier than I had hoped.

Near Meerut there is a shrine where a renowned mystic – Sheikh Pir Shattari – is buried, and who died here in 1632. He is extremely important because he was one of the *Shattaris*, the mystics who practised a special form of concentration which was believed to produce a complete change in the disciple and perhaps make him also into a teacher in an incredibly short period of time. Callandars, I discovered, often visited this shrine : sometimes in disguise, sometimes not. I had chosen Spin Dil to travel with me partly because in Kashmir he had been the disciple of a Sufi teacher, and was familiar with the way of thinking whose exponents I was seeking. He and I went to see a local resident who was reputed to be something of a magician and bore the name of 'Sufi', in addition to a great deal of other appellations, in the luxuriant fashion of the Indian Moslems.

He was of noble Mogul blood, a retired former member of the Indian Civil Service, living in fair comfort with a large house and mango-orchard, and he welcomed us as something which would break the monotony of a life which did not change very much from day to day. I shall call him Akbar Baig. He was able to clear up quite a number of questions which had puzzled me about Sufism since I first made contact with it in Pakistan. He was not a member of any Order (there are said to be seventy-six of them) but had studied under a number of teachers, and had read a great deal in the original Arabic and Persian as well as in English, which he spoke with immense fluency and an atrocious accent.

The study of the Sufis, he told me, was made more difficult than anything should be by the fact that the teacher has to approach his disciple in a way which the disciple will understand. He is teaching something – a spiritual discipline – which has little in common with ordinary life. It was true that the Sufis saw all life as a part of a process, and the physical and spiritual as one continuum; but their inner experiences bore only an approximate relationship to normal human ones. 'How, then, is the Sufi to explain all in a coherent system, when what he tells and does is of another dimension?'

71

The difficulty was very real. 'The Sufis do not,' said Akbar, his bald head wagging with emphasis, 'they do not, I say, always suffer fools gladly. Then there is another thing: they cannot offer a cut-and-dried plan for you to study, as you can in other methods. This is because the cut-and-dried plan is always an imitation, or a part of the whole teaching. It is used by people who follow a limited or theoretical school.'

I steered him onto the subject of the Callandars. 'Yes, yes. They are mystics, and they are Sufis. But you see, they are only Callandars when they are in a certain period of their lives. They may die as Callandars, and then they are revered and shrines may be put up to them. But generally to be a Callandar is only a phase in the life of a Sufi.' Could I meet a Callandar?

'I will try to arrange it, but I do not know. They don't need anything, you see, and we cannot extend such inducements as would be applicable elsewhere.' In spite of his amateur interest in the mystic way of the Sufi, I could still descry the terminology of the I.C.S. breaking through.

I was staying at a former British club, with all the marks and many of the routines of its former imperial glory. Some days later, when I went out onto the verandah for my early morning tea, I found the Callandar on the lawn. He was dressed in a rough robe of cotton, with bare feet and head. His cranium was completely shaved. For one crazy moment, through association of ideas, I thought that this baldpate with the mug in his hand and staff by his side was Akbar Baig himself. Unfortunately for the drama of the tale, it was not – not even his brother, except in the wildest possible sense. He must have seen me at about the same moment. I waved to him, feeling rather foolish, and he raised one arm, after describing a rough circle with it, then without further invitation, he rose, picked up his paraphernalia, and stalked up to me. I took his hand as he climbed onto the balcony. From his shoulder he unlooped a small fur rug, and sat down on it. I noticed that the whole of the head was shaved; not only the pate, moustache and beard, but the eyebrows as well. This Callandar, at any rate, did not seem to be in disguise. If he was, he was disguised as a Callandar.

I called for more tea, rather to the unease of the waiter, and waited for the visitor to speak. He smiled, showing two rows of very even teeth, and smoothed his blue robe. So I started to ask

him how he was : *Apka mizaji mubarak kaisa hai?* This did not
seem to be greatly to his liking, for he answered, almost without
a pause, in a low but strangely-accented voice, what I took to
be : *Ap ap hai mizaj hai, kaisa kaisa hai.* This might be freely
translated as 'It all depends what you mean by "How are you?" '
Literally it means : 'You are you, health is health, how is how.'

Communication was finally established in a mixture of Persian
and English, with the preference for the former. First, he said,
in answer to my question, he would tell me nothing about himself. He was not interested, either, in what I had to say about
myself, or who had taught me what and when.

'I have come here to tell you things. I have not come here to
be inspected or judged by you. You cannot do that, because you
lack the necessary knowledge.'

All this, I must add, was said in the politest possible way,
and sounded far less jarring to the ego than it may when written
down.

He had, however, evidently heard what it was that I wanted
to know. He now told me that the original decision to found the
Callandars was made in Turkestan, that the teaching was collected by a Sayed (a descendant of Mohammed) who came to
Delhi and taught the 'work' to certain disciples. Callandars were
not connected with Hindus, who only trained people, did not
teach them. Some Hindus were more enlightened, but these
did not teach. All Yoga was a form of self-deception and could
easily be learned. The Callandars did not teach when they were
in a 'condition of callandarism', but learned and served during
this period, were perfecting themselves. While he was gulping
his tea from his own mug, I found out how to steer the conversation in the direction I wanted. I realised that I could
not ask any question; but I remembered that in the community of Kunjizagh where I had attended sessions, the master
could be prompted or questioned by merely saying a word :
without any interrogative inflection. The other method was to
make a signal with the hand, but this was allowed only to people
of advanced degree. So I said, in as level a tone as possible :
'Insani Kamil' (the Perfected Man).

He took me up at once, putting the mug down on the boards
beside him. *'Insani Kamil* means someone who is completed.
We all strive for completeness; but we have first to learn how

to strive. This is your problem. This is, in fact, all that a teacher will ever be able to teach you. When you have learned this, you will be on the way to becoming *Insani Kamil*'.

Again I spoke: '*Latayif*'. This is a technical term with the Sufis, and refers to certain areas of the body which are thought to have a greater potential affinity with the spiritual than other parts. The Callander came to life in a strange way.

'The illumination of the *Latayif* is the way to completion.' His eyes were gleaming, and he waved his arms in the air. 'No sage who does not teach the method of making these secret areas of the body full of power can ever be your guide.'

Then he stood up, made over his breast with his right hand the rapid elliptical sign that I had first noted, and left me, climbing over the verandah and striding away out of my life.

I met another sort of Callandar when I returned to Delhi, through a friend of the resourceful Spin Dil. He was between thirty and forty years of age, half Persian and working in a bank. He showed me a picture of one of the greatest Callandar teachers, who had had, of course, to go through the whole of the callandarist austerities before he became a sage. The sage's anniversary had just been celebrated throughout India, but I had missed it. The picture showed a man plentifully endowed with facial hair ('he grew it after he had completed his callandari') sitting on a tiger-skin rug with his hands upraised, the fingers linked together. Only the lower part of the body is covered, with a white cloth. The superscription reads: 'The Blessed Presence Bu Ali Shah, Callandar, Year 1100 Hijri.' He was originally the Mufti of Delhi, but abandoned scholarship after being rebuked by a fakir who told him that he was undeveloped in the true sense. My young Callandar friend, Imtiaz, explained why such fragmentary accounts of the dervishes are all that one can generally obtain without tremendous trouble in travel and study.

'A mystic of our Order,' he said, 'and this goes for most of the other ones as well, may not reveal anything to initiates except that part of the Path in which he is completely well versed. In the case of non-initiates, one has to talk almost in another language, because the resources of normal speech are simply not able to convey experiences which are not like anything that the ordinary person undergoes in life.'

I asked him whether it would not be possible to piece together, from various accounts, something of the essence of the path which is generally called Sufic. 'Only if you had been initiated by a large number of different people; and if you have been taken in certain directions by each of them; and then find that you can put all this down on paper – then, perhaps. But it will never happen.'

Why was that? 'Because, as should be obvious to you, your teacher will introduce you to the Path in the way best suited to you; then the next one will take on where the first left off. So one person cannot gain the truth through dabbling.'

I wondered, almost aloud, what this young man hoped to gain from practices which did not seem to belong to the kind of modern life which he lived, in a tiny apartment, surrounded by English books – and a Hindi grammar. He told me. 'The Callandar path entwines with many other paths. One such path is the path of modern life. The man who has the key to this is a teacher. It is from such teachers that the future development of man will come.'

Did he feel that the Callandars were doing something which would influence the East and the West; or how would the transformation which all the mystics I had met were talking about, actually take place? 'If one actually *knew*,' he told me, 'in the real sense of knowing a thing – it would have happened already. Religious people find that faith is difficult for them, from time to time. We are only a little better. For us there is a sense of certainty that this transformation will take place. For my own part, I am sure that it will take place in the West. But it must be kept going in the East – even if only for our own sake. Even,' he added, as if in afterthought, 'if it is only that we have to keep a lamp alight here for people to take flame from.'

He introduced me to his uncle, who had little to add, except that I should see a group of Callandars, for 'life consists of bodies of people, not single ones.' They invited me to meet their friends, who assembled once a week in the basement of a store which had been put at their disposal by a wealthy supporter. I went there two nights later, with Spin Dil and Imtiaz.

A man stood at the door, looking rather closely at everyone who sought admission. Imtiaz struck the ground with his stick and was allowed in. A moment later we joined him. In the centre of the cemented floor sat a dozen Callanders, only three of whom had shaven heads and faces. Around the walls of the cellar were about fifty other people, of various ages, and including children. They all seemed to be middle-class Indians, probably Moslems. The place was fitfully lighted by mosque lamps suspended from the ceiling. It was apparent that a meal had just taken place, and the night's activities were about to start.

The leader was a thin man, middle-aged, dressed in a loose white robe which he seemed somehow unaccustomed to wearing. He stood up, and there was a hush from the dervishes, who stopped moving from side to side. The leader addressed them in Persian, which I was able to follow quite well. It was the language of the classics – of Saadi, Rumi, Jami, Khayyam – and not the sing-song affectation which is used in Iran today. As usual, he was saying, the proceedings would take the form of a moment of concentration – 'remembering' – a moment of action; and a moment of listening.

These 'moments' varied in length, and were organised by the teacher. First, at a signal – the shouted word *hoo*! – the Callandars started a series of movements; sometimes complex, sometimes simple, they did not move in unison but in order. They were sitting in a double line on their fur rugs, facing one another. As they moved I heard first the beat of a small drum from the darkness, then the thin trill of flute music which seemed to weave in and out of the beat. Presently a voice began to sing. This, quite certainly, was the form of dance used by the Callandars. The effect was peaceful and pleasing for the audience, which visibly relaxed; though the Callandars were having a hard time of it. As far as I could see, there was not one without sweat on his face. But the exercise continued for what seemed a very considerable period. Then, in mid-movement, the chief called sharply and decisively two words. All movement stopped.

There was complete silence from the Callandars. They simply sat there, immobile, impassive, their faces showing no sign of life. This must be the 'moment' of remembering. All at once the lips of the mystics began to move, as if they were in a very great hurry to finish some recitation before yet another signal. I expected another interruption, but there was none. The lips moved more and more slowly. Then all was immobility again. The 'moment' of remembering did not come in the order in which it had been announced: but this may have been for a good reason.

Now came the 'moment' of listening, corresponding with what other dervishes call 'audition'. It is a strange experience even when one is hearing it for the first time in Western surroundings from a tape-recorder; because it is the impact of sound which has no perceptible rhythm for the most part. First a voice starts repeating phrases. Some of them can be understood, some not. Then a musical instrument breaks in with an unearthly sound. As this fades the drum starts rapping, almost like a spiritualist phenomenon. I recognised the Callandar 'moment' of listening from something which had been played for me in Cairo. At that time the amiable Turk who operated the tape-recorder had asked me whether I knew what it was; and claimed that he 'found it on the machine when he bought it.' I now began to think that he had been testing me for some purpose of his own. All the more so because I had been over-enthusiastically introduced to him as something of an expert on the Sufis. The moment of listening, according to the luminous hands of my watch, had lasted for sixteen minutes when the immobile group started to move again. In spite of the confusing interchange of sounds – vocal, percussive and musical – they did not try to adjust themselves to it, as would have seemed necessary. Instead they were performing rhythmic movements of a strange sort, with their arms and legs. Imtiaz, I now noticed, was quite near to me in the second Callandar file, and I could see that his eyes blinked with the movements. When there was a pause, the eyes would remain open or shut, according to how they had been at the instant the movement ceased.

Spin Dil, at my elbow and with his back to the wall like the rest of the spectators, touched my arm. I moved towards him. 'You can talk if you wish,' he said, 'they will not be disturbed.' I noted that the Indian audience, unlike any other Indian audience I had ever seen, were so quiet that one would not have known that they were there. Nobody spat, chewed *paan,* scratched himself, cleared his throat, or even cried *shabash*!

I asked Spin Dil how long the session lasted. 'this all depends upon the Badshah (Monarch),' he said, gesturing towards the leader of the Callandars. 'What are your own feelings about this?' I told him that I did not know. It seemed to me to resemble in certain ways the Sufi procedures which I had seen elsewhere. That was all.

'That is all it is,' he replied.

Suddenly I felt cold. It was, indeed, very cold in that cellar, in spite of the amount of heat which must have been generated by the performers. And, almost as soon as the thought came into my head, the leader clapped his hands, and the meeting broke up.

Imtiaz and his uncle joined us and brought the Badshah with them. He shook hands perfunctorily, like a bored business executive. I now saw that he was wearing glasses and had a scholarly stoop. 'Come to my home, for it is late' he said, and bundled us out through the silently dispersing dervishes towards a small car which was parked outside.

The chief Callandar was, of all things, a newspaper proprietor. He took us to a well-appointed little house in the newer part of the capital, ablaze with light, furnished in a most contemporary style. Here, after removing our shoes in order not to spoil our host's Kashan rugs, we were soon settled in a comfortable room, decorated with Persian miniatures of the Mogul School.

The Badshah was, like many Indian Moslems, of part Mogul stock and very well mannered indeed. I told him at once that I was interested to see and learn as much as possible about the various dervish orders before the old ways died out. There was, I said, very little literature on this subject in Europe or America. I was also very much interested in the theme that a 'superior man' was being created by dervish methods.

'In the first place,' he said, suddenly grave, 'the dervishes are not being swallowed up or dying out. Much of the picturesqueness which you associate with them is passing, it is true. But the *work* – as we call it – of the dervish is penetrating into a different medium. This is because of the evolution of society. Secondly, you may be compelled by being Western to concentrate upon the theme of 'perfecting man'.

'You should know that among us this comes *after* actual experience. After all, when one has no idea as to what a 'perfected man' may be like, how and why should one try to become one? If you try to 'Westernise' the procedures of the dervishes, you will get no further than the yogis who have 'Easternised' some of them. They are out on one limb : you will be out on another.'

I could see his point; but I wanted to know what the angle of approach of the Westerner should be in that case. 'It is something more subtle than you are accustomed to thinking,' he said at once. 'You see a man, talk to him – and you realise that he can teach you. This is your man. Perhaps you have been told about him and then meet him. But you have to be very careful because there are a great many semi-teachers. These are not all frauds, like some of the people who peddle compact philosophies in the West. But there is a severe limitation on what they teach. At a certain point you must lose touch with them, deliberately.'

Could he be more explicit? He could, and was. 'In other schools there is hostility towards another form of teaching. We Sufis do not have this. Anyone may benefit from anything. "It is an ill wind" as you say. But there is a much more important point. You see among Sufis *the teacher himself is taught to be a teacher.*' He repeated this accentuated phrase three times, as he looked at me.

'And when a man teaches our Way, he will always have one, or two, of his disciples who become fully-fledged teachers as a result. They do not just set themselves up as teachers.'

'Badshah,' I said, 'I have met a great number of Sufis now, from Pakistan in the East to Morocco in the West. And, as you probably know, there are quite a number of people teaching "occult" and similar semi-religious practises in the West. How do you view these people?'

The Badshah smiled. 'There are undesirable teachers in the East as well as the West. The only test which you can apply, unless you know instinctively, is that the real teacher is uncompromising. He appears to the "unripe" to be stern, to take no interest in things that the outsider thinks are important. He is, above all, a man not afraid. Not afraid in small things, not afraid in large ones. We have fewer teachers than you may think; and plenty of practitioners. Your real teacher will tell you things; not ask you things. He will not ask you to believe things; he will present things to you. Your progress will then be up to you.'

'The answer to that,' I told him, 'is that I fear that people of your persuasion will gain little progress in the West as a whole.

Our heritage is that we think for ourselves. We claim the right to evaluate evidence through the power of our own intelligence and reason. This is the Western way.'

'I won't ask you where it has got you' said the Badshah, 'all this "reason". But I will tell you that you people have far more *faith* than you realise. This is why you talk so much of "reason". The faith is there, waiting to come out. And come out it will, when it is ready – not when you think you are ready.'

We went out into the garden, pacing among brilliant flowers and cunningly-contrived rockeries which seemed to fill an immense space, so economically had the area been used. It was only when I was outside its walls that I realised how small it really was, and how I would not even have suspected its existence behind the thirty-foot stone buttresses which concealed it and the house. One could have passed through those dusty lanes a hundred times and never found the garden of the Badshah.

A line of lanterns had been placed along the side of an artificial pool, and as we peered at the carp and pieces of coral in its depths, a white cloth was brought by three disciples and placed upon the ground for us to eat our evening meal.

As we sat down, more disciples joined us, until there were thirty there. They shared all the tasks, passing great plates of chicken pilau and yoghurt from one hand to the next. In spite of much practice, I felt rather cramped sitting on the grass with my feet under me. But I had a place of honour, next to the teacher. He read my thoughts about the disciples. As I was about to ask about them he said : 'We are all brothers here. These men whom you see attending me and serving one another, they all have their own homes. We rotate duties. Sometimes we have the meal at their houses, a different one each time. Tonight, as it happens, most of the men here are of the middle class, as you would call it. But, just as you saw us with the poorest people at the Zikr-meeting, so you see people more important than me here tonight, working as servants. You *preach* equality in the West. We, here, practise it. But it is easier for us – we have had much more time to learn.'

At that very moment a youth of about twenty came in to the garden and placed his hand on his heart. The Badshah, without a moment's hesitation, jumped up and ran to him, kissing his hand and placing it to his head. He brought him back to where

I was sitting, and sat him at his right hand.

'This boy,' said the Badshah, pointing to the newcomer, who seemed to me to be no more extraordinary than anyone else, 'this boy is of the very highest rank in the Way.'

'I suppose,' I said 'that those who cannot recognise the masters often pass them in the street, as it were.'

The Badshah smiled. 'If there is anything true, it is that.' I stayed three days with the newspaper magnate. He taught me a series of callisthenic exercises which were a part of the Callandars' traditional health lore, described a number of medicinal plants which were reputed to cure all manner of ills, took me to see various groups of Sufis whose practices were 'never to be repeated to anyone.' It was, in spite of my previous contact with Sufis, like stepping into another world. When we were with Hindus or people from another background, at the races, in the office, or in a restaurant – and the Badshah had many friends – there was never a suggestion of Callandarism. Conversations were about almost every topic under the sun.

This really is one of the strangest things about the Sufis. All other mystics seem to have a formalised, 'professional' attitude towards their vocation, as if they were trained to it. Sufis are Sufis – and – also whatever else they are expected to be.

There was never any of the awkwardness with these men of God which one would feel with a priest of any other persuasion from time to time. And yet there was no doubt in my mind that they were genuinely spiritual people, and in a very deep sense. This could almost be called the baffling characteristic of the Sufis – and it is also one of their most endearing ones. Spirituality is a part of their nature, as if it has seeped into the very texture of their being. They are not living a special kind of life; they are living life, and being Sufis is completely compatible with it.

This tendency was especially striking when contrasted with the Hindu religious man, who tends to be self-conscious, as if he is afraid somewhere deep down inside that he is not spiritual at all.

CHAPTER SIX

The Fakirs

India is equated in many minds with mystery and magic, with occultism and hidden truth. This idea carried with it the feeling that somewhere here, in this enormous land which is really a continent, almost a world of its own, are to be found the origins of truth, or at least of spiritually important things. Some have sought enlightenment through actual contact with Indian mystics; others through a study of the immensely rich religious literature of the Hindu and others.

On closer study the picture of India as the source of even its own mystical tradition presents a very different aspect. The history of the aborigines, the dark-skinned, almost black Dravidians, is a closed book. Hinduism has undoubtedly absorbed many customs and beliefs from the earlier inhabitants – and vice-versa. But the Vedic hymns of the Hindus, with their mystical and magical extensions, are now known to have been composed in Central Asia, and to have been brought by the Hindus, an immigrant race, to the country of 'Holy Mother Ganges' – the river which could not have been a holy mother to the original Hindus at all. If we are looking for origins, it is to Central Asia that we must look for the genesis, or at least very early development, of the Indian mystical way.

To what extent was the secret, occult tradition of the Hindus transplanted when the Aryan hordes brought their cattle to graze on the fair plains of Hindustan? The tradition, it is true, became naturalised, an Indian tradition. It became divided into several schools of religious thought and practice, coalesced into more or less rigid training-systems, which were believed to produce in the practitioner psychic phenomena, occult powers, contact with deity and the rest. But there was another factor which complicated the issue. The Hinduism of old Aryana in Central Asia may have been centred around ecstatogenic processes, or it may not. The Hindus, in leaving their ancient homeland, may have left the geographical centre of their teachings, but they did not free themselves from what might be called 'mystical interchange'. It is a fair assumption that the traditional Afghan stories which speak of continuous contact between India and ancient 'Ariana' (of which modern Afghanistan is a part) and hence light is shed on the ancient theory that mystical activity once established somewhere continues to exercise an attraction. In addition to this, there is the refreshing of the tradition from its source.

However this may be, in more modern times we find the constant flowing into India of the Sufi mystics from Afghanistan and other parts of Central Asia. Today there is much less communication, because of the coming into being of Pakistan between the two countries. But in the past what Pir Zamin Nizami calls the 'magnetic pull' of the Central Asian mystics, most of the Sufis, exercised an almost unbelievable effect upon the ascetics and mystics of the Indian continent.

The list of Sufi shrines and circles in India, even in predominantly Hindu areas, is without end, and could never be compiled. In a country which was never fully brought under the sway of Islam, every corner of India has its Sufi centre. This is not to say that such centres represent the 'magnetism' of the Sufi teacher who founded them. On the contrary, the tendency has been for cults to grow up which sometimes make the Sufi congeries look like collections of Hindu *sadhus;* even if many Hindu *gurus* early took the Sufi appellation of *Fakir* and applied it to themselves.

But where the branch is, the root must be found. In spite of the fact that some of the most notable Sufis of all time are buried on Indian soil, their graves being centres of pilgrimage for of all faiths, it is ultimately to the lands beyond the Khyber that the adherents of these teachers look for the continuing source of their inspiration.

That the incredibly difficult terrain and uncertain intentions of the average Afghan towards the heterodox should have allowed centres of pilgrimage and teaching to flourish in their country is surprising enough. That, in this century when the Westernised town-dwellers of Afghanistan generally tend to oppose such medieval survivals as mysticism, Hindu India has a strong emotional affection towards Moslem Afghanistan is partly due to a half-remembered heart-call to their spiritual centre. Talk to any Hindu, and you will instantly find that warmth for Afghanistan which, in all conscience, one would hardly expect towards a people who have, with Islamic zeal, invaded the land of the gentle Hindu time and again and ruled it without invariable mercy.

A famous Indian poetess, Prabhjjot, composed an ode of welcome to the Afghan king when he visited India in 1958. Among the lines were these, widely repeated and publicised:

'The seekers of truth look at one another
The same soul pervades, what if the colours are different?
The tradition of the Vedas is felt afresh.
The world has changed and the people have become strong,
Asia is a big continent and Afghanistan is like its heart'.

This bond between the two areas, which have taken such very different paths of evolution, seems to be the only key to the study of the development of Sufism in India, and the coalition of the Fakir phenomenon which I was studying.

Travelling in India before actually seeking sources in Afghanistan, I was able to see the interplay of rites and practices in the Indian field. This was an immense help to understanding the origins of large parts of the cults when I eventually penetrated to the Afghan uplands. Afterwards I became convinced that to study the Sufis in India on their own is like trying to identify a sheep by looking at a ball of wool. Investigating the literature of Sufism is little better, because of the special uses of the Sufi writings, which are not intended to be read all through like an ordinary book.

Like the more native cults of the Hindus, Indian Sufi communities are usually grouped around the personality or legend of a master-teacher, and one who came from Central Asia for preference. There is a tendency towards fragmentation, with disciples setting up their own cults here and there, for a number of reasons; sometimes for no visible reason at all. What is most striking is that the complicated exercise of the Central Asians – in which music, rhythm and thought are combined – have been subdivided by Indian Sufis. This means that one group will practise, say, listening to music alternating with concentration, as a method of entering the 'mystical state'; another will experiment with telepathy and the repetition of religious formulae; yet others will seem to be indulging in magic or displays of self-mortification.

In this, the scattered Sufis of India resemble their Hindu neighbours to a striking degree. The Yoga postures and the *chakras* (physically located spiritual centres of the body) which some Hindus concern themselves with, are paralleled by similar activities by the Sufi orders. Breathing exercises and ritualistic observances of closely similar type are found in the two cultures side by side. The Indian tendency, then, is to concentrate upon a restricted number of techniques to produce the mystical effect; while the Central Asian one regards almost every movement, thought or impact to be significant in the development of man.

I visited a musical evening of a group of Chishti fakirs, who seemed to pass into a sort of trance by listening to various instruments being played. This is an important Order in India, and I got to know some of its members very well. Although they are themselves convinced that in the trance-state they attain a form of 'liberation' or divine contact, I showed that this state (*hal*) could be produced in them merely by suggestion. It was possible to produce the sensation even in members who, after a number of years' listening or playing instruments, had been unable to attain it. Some of the less well-informed members of one Chishti circle began to regard me as a magician; others claimed that I had 'special gifts' which I did not myself understand. This was no experimental result, they said, capable of being duplicated almost at will. Whether I knew it or not, my activities were divinely ordained by a greater Fate than anyone understood, for the special purpose of bringing this knowledge to the Chishties.

By other standards many of the Indian Sufis were not Sufis at all. Some of them adhered to a policy of strict hostility towards Hinduism and a fanatical attachment to Islam which was merely emotional. This they considered to be a divine gift; they had been shown the 'only true Way'. Others, notably in a small town where Moslems and Hindus were about evenly represented, thought that Sufism was a sort of instrument for producing concord between members of rival religions. They held frequent meetings during which they produced quotations from their scriptures and those of other people, designed to show the essential identity of religion. When I told them that according to what I had learned, the essential truth did not consist of parallel slogans, they thought that I was a troublemaker.

One fakir, whose whole family – some fourteen people – were all practising healers and general mystical advisers, came to me and offered to display his prowess. He performed the trick of making a mango-plant 'grow' in a few minutes from a mango-stone, and I rewarded him accordingly. He was a Hindu, and when I had said that I was not really interested in conjuring, he said: 'Neither am I, but I do this in order to interest people, and keep up my reputation.' Although to all outward appearance a fully-fledged fakir, he was in fact a disciple of a Sufi teacher, whose meetings he attended secretly, so as not to 'lose caste'.

The search for the perfect man, or the production of the New Man, which I was later to find strongly marked in the Central Asian schools, and which preoccupied Western Sufis like the Moroccans, was only dimly recognised here as an objective. Almost all had heard of it, it is true, but they regarded this branch of Sufi effort as 'something very high'. Generally when I mentioned this subject I was referred to the old writers, such as Rumi, Jili, al-Ghazzali, and told that only high initiates knew what it meant.

An exception was a Naqshbandi sheikh, who traced his 'spiritual pedigree' back nearly fourteen hundred years, and believed himself to be inspired by the essence or inner reality of all the great Sufi teachers. 'The Sufi teacher' he said, 'is one, even though he may seem to be ten thousand. There is, in fact, only one Sufi teacher, in many seeming bodies.'

Sheikh Hawaili's feeling was that man must perfect himself, and that this was the reason for his presence upon earth. Everything which happened to him, every thought, every action which affected him, had a constructive or destructive effect upon this evolutionary process. The only way to preserve the 'right road' was to act in accordance with instant instinct, to react to situations as they developed. This could only be done by those who had developed within them the consciousness that they possessed a superior power.

This superior power could be said to reside in the five sensitive areas of the body, which were reflected in the mind. It is towards the activating of these centres that the Fakir's life is dedicated. Until these have been made sensitive, no further progress can be made. Once they are sensitised, they act as one organ, and this is the spiritual organ which determines man's development. Man, he said, would never develop any further physically: rather he would deteriorate unless he kept up his physical fitness. The body, having reached its apogee, would destroy the mind, unless the mind were made alert to its responsibilities, reformed, regenerated and in turn revivified the body. Then the mind and the body would constitute one organ, and this is what the Perfect Man actually meant.

The sheikh concentrated upon awakening the secret organ. This was done through exercises and repetitions. I saw a number of young men carrying on these techniques, and was allowed to take part in them. 'What happens,' I asked him, 'when some progress has been made, and one of the five organs which are destined to become one organ is activated?'

'Then I send the man away, to activate the next one with another teacher,' he said; 'this prevents attachment to my personality alone, and allows the system to be diffused throughout the body of the Naqshbandi community.'

This pattern of thought and training, I was to find in Central Asia, was closer to the non-Indian methodology than any other. When he was a young man the Sheikh had studied in Bokhara. He could not, or would not, tell me much about the Afghan Sufis. I showed him evidence of my initiation, and mentioned the community at Kunji Zagh. 'In that case,' he said, 'you must remain within your own discipline.'

He and others later confirmed that Kafiristan in the Hindu Kush eastern ranges was the place where what might be called a comprehensive form of Sufi teaching was carried out. I wanted to make my way there with as little delay as possible, but in the first place much of the territory was snowbound, and I had next to no knowledge about it. I had heard from people who had been to Afghanistan that conditions there were not such as to allow stray foreigners to wander all over the country. Even Afghans themselves did not often go to Kafiristan. It remained the country of a little-known people, even if it was located within the boundaries of a developing State.

All countries have their peculiarities, and one of the characteristics of Afghanistan is to weave a spell over the heart and mind of those who travel there. The roads are often bad, the people generally pursue their own ways without much regard for the foreigner in their midst, there are shortages of all sorts of commodities which are a part of everyday life elsewhere. Even the Afghan is a creature of infinite variety : he may be a Pathan, a Mongol, an Arab or a Kafir. He may, again, be something else. He may not speak the same language as the man in the next village; some of his newspapers are printed in a language that only a minority understands. But Afghanistan is a magic land, and there is no getting away from that.

The very name conjures up visions of the Khyber Pass, of Central Asian nomads, of wild Fakirs, of the buffer-state and crossroads of Asia which Kipling immortalised for generations of English readers. In three wars the British and the Afghans have measured swords : the last one being a brief affair in 1919. But there is very much more to Afghanistan than even this. This is the land where, some scholars think, Zoroaster may have lived; where the early Hindu scriptures were composed. It was the birthplace of Babur, the first of the Mogul emperors of India, and the heartland of Mahmud of Ghazna, the terrible conqueror whose operations beyond the Indus gave him a name which Hindu mothers still use to frighten their children. Vestiges of all these factors are still to be found, in the archaeology and in the life of the Afghan people.

One of the most baffling things I learned from reports about Afghanistan is that, without contacts, without keeping yourself abreast of developments through a sort of personal intelligence service, you have almost no idea as to what is going on. True, you have the radio and the newspapers. They will tell you something, but seldom anything of interest to the traveller or the explorer. Although there is a certain amount of preoccupation with the country's history and archaeology, the general attitude of the Afghan is that one should be impressed by the modern developments; the irrigation schemes, the unveiling of the women, the striding into the twentieth century. Afghanistan's history, described by one authority as 'the richest treasure in all Asia' is too often looked upon by the proud official as something which has to be pressed into service in order to impress the visitor with the importance of the present-day nation.

It is necessary to mention these things in order to give some sort of reason for the barrier which officialdom erects between the foreigner and the country; between department and department; between one man and the next. Hence the need for the national 'grapevine', which the general populace continues to use, as one Afghan told me, 'as we have for generations. There is always a government which is mainly intent upon remaining in power. So the people just carry on in their own sweet way.' This way is to collect information, as automatically as the housewife talking over her garden fence absorbs all the trivia from her neighbour which will enable her to piece together a complete picture of life in the next house.

It is not necessary to consider that the official attitude is in any way wrong, just because it differs from the one to which we have been accustomed. It is easy to criticise if one does not know the problems which the administration has to face; and the hardy, proud Afghans are by no means dismayed by the behaviour which they accept and expect in their rulers. What is rather absurd is the pretence that this curious invidiousness is not there at all; that all is straightforward, simple, plain and progressive. When the Afghan knows you well, he will talk fairly freely in front of you, and you will see his 'private face' as clearly as his public one. He loves his country with a fervour which I have not seen surpassed. He will go to almost any lengths to conceal something which is detrimental to its *abru,* its honour. When the demand for a separate State for the Pathans became woven into the *abru*-sense of the Afghans, it ceased to be a matter which could be considered merely a clash of government. This kind of feeling has to be experienced (or at least seen at close quarters) to be understood.

Plenty of people travel through Afghanistan. They generally enter from the Persian border, and traverse the country via motor-roads to Kabul, and then on through the Khyber to Pakistan. This succession of vehicles, ranging from air-conditioned trucks carrying well-equipped expeditions to the flimsiest of motorised cycles, is referred to by the Afghans as the *Karawani-Kitabnavisan* – the Caravan of Writers – or, less complimentarily, as the *se-roz-yak-kitab* (three days one book) referring to the fact that everyone passing this way seems to be writing a travel book.

But the difficulties of getting anywhere in Afghanistan, especially to see people whom one wants to see, are immense. In the first place, a large number of areas are considered to be military zones. In the second people asking to go to one place often find themselves being 'sold' another. Some say that this is due to spy-fever; others that the officials tend to think that you, as a stranger, do not really know where you want to go, and they can advise better. From the frozen wastes and truly towering mountains of the north-east to the salt deserts of the south-west, Afghanistan is such a medley of races and terrain that most people manage to see only one or two places, to get a whiff of the atmosphere, a 'lift' through the truly magnificent hospitality of the people – and . . . out.

Kafiristan has never been properly explored. Until Victorian times it was a no-man's land, unclaimed by anyone at all because it was so inaccessible. Extending through a mountainous area as wild as any on the earth's surface, it was the home of the oldest people in Afghanistan : both in terms of years and history. It was thought, and it seems likely, that these people were there long before the Graeco-Buddhists who were displaced by the Moslem invasion. When the Arabs over-ran Afghanistan, some of the Buddhists and others fled into the truly inaccessible north-east, and settled among the Kafirs – the 'infidels'.

The King of Kabul (Afghanistan was not a united state then) at the end of the last century invaded Kafiristan and brought the 'light of Islam to the heathen', after an incredibly hard winter campaign. And so it was renamed the Country of Light. Although some accessible parts of the country are open to visitors, the main part of it is almost never visited except by pilgrims and others who have business there. To the modern Afghan it is something of an enigma : and also, of course, a disgrace that such a 'primitive' people should exist within the borders of their progressive state.

My interest in Kafiristan was specific. I knew that Afghanistan had been a centre of Buddhist learning and pilgrimage long before there was such a thing as a Dalai or a Panchen Lama in Tibet. Indeed, Tibet took the place of Afghanistan after the latter country was Islamised and the huge sanctuary of Bamian was overwhelmed in the seventh century. According to tradition, the monks of Afghanistan fled to Kafiristan. Some took the road to Tibet, others remained and started their schools of meditation anew in the land of the infidels. The Buddhism of China and Japan today is derived from the Afghan Bamian monastery-complex as evidenced by sculptures still extant.

Some of this information I had obtained from Sufi mystics and others in India, where there were any number of Tibetan refugees. One could go to Tibet to seek refugee Buddhists from the Kafir area – or their descendants. The country was under the Chinese communists. In any case there would be little left in the monasteries to study; and few lamas would be found there now. Before Kafiristan became Westernised, there was a chance that something might be found.

A friend in a Government department put me in touch with some of the Dalai Lama's satellites, and after that the picture became a little clearer. Tibet, according to these experts, was not actually cut off from the 'West', even if only because refugees continued to arrive. There were Moslems living in Tibet, and had been for a great many years. Some of them were Indian citizens, spoke Tibetan, and should be able to advise me further. These Buddhist gentlemen, with gratifyingly little sectarianism in their makeup, told me something about the Sufi practices which they had heard of in Tibet: but they told me nothing new. Jalu Kambo was my man, it seemed, for he was a 'very mystical Momatan' (Mohammedan) who knew Lhasa and other parts of Tibet.

Jalu was the charming contraction of the more formidable Jalaluddin (glory of the Faith) and he was part-Turkoman, part-Tibetan, a trader formerly of Lhasa, now by some alchemy an Indian. And without him I could not have got the picture clearly. He was fat, forty and benign, spoke English well, seemed to take a great liking to me. But I often felt that he thought that I was involved in some kind of anti-Communist intelligence work. In fact, he almost begged me to confide it to him; for he could help me to make contacts to help throw the hated Chinese out 'when it was time'.

'When it is time, Omo Sahib, they will be thrown out. And I will help. Please let me help.' When I had to some extent convinced him that I was after Sufis, and studying practical mysticism of this particular school, he admitted defeat. 'You do not want Tibet at all,' he said, sorrowfully. 'The Mother-house of the Soo-fee-aaa is not in Tibet. You find the mother-house, because they will only send you to the mother-house if you go to Lhasa.' And where was the mother-house?

'Hindu-killer mountains, eastwards, past the Khajakhel, in Afghanistan.' Afghanistan was, if anything, as tricky as Tibet. Or perhaps it was because I now knew something about the Afghans, and very little about the Tibetans.

Jalu's geography might have been sketchy, but what he said did undoubtedly mean Kafiristan. So I headed for Pakistan again, to collect information as to how a one-man expedition might penetrate through two main screens: the official and non-official curiosity, and the mountains of Kafiristan itself. Not to mention the Kafirs, a completely unknown quantity.

I had to see people in Karachi, Rawalpindi and Peshawar before I had pieced together enough to apply any sort of reasoning to the project. Some of the information which I got from people who had been to Afghanistan was gloomy. 'Once within the Afghan kingdom, and you are trapped,' said one European. 'The country is ruled by what may be a benevolent regime, it may be paternalistic and neutralist. But it knows what it is doing, and you cannot travel where you will. Military reasons, of course.' He tried to draw me out, in that desultory way familiar to all old India hands, to see whether I had a special mission of some kind.

A Pakistani official told me: 'Endless delays in getting permission to visit certain areas are the order of the day. As you have been in Pakistan, you will not be welcome at all,' 'Even in Kabul,' said a diplomat from a foreign Embassy, 'diplomatists are often kept posted as to the latest news by their servants. At diplomatic receptions and cocktail parties they avidly try to pick one anothers' brains for any titbit to send home.'

I spoke to Pakistani citizens who travelled to and from Kabul on business and for other purposes. Those who were not involved in political matters confirmed that the place was difficult to travel in; that gossip provided most of the general information; that if I told anyone that I wanted to go to Kafiristan, I would be 'given the run-around' – and would get nowhere.

Through my Sufi sources, I heard a great deal more. There was not only a way into and out of Afghanistan – there were many ways. This system was called the *rahi-gurez* (escape route), used by smugglers of men and materials of all kinds,. including arms. Kafiristan, according to the Sufis, was the home of the esoteric school called the Sarmoon, the occult branch of the

Nakshibandi Order of Bokhara. This was a school which formerly had branches all over the Moslem world. Even today they are quite widespread, but the yoga-like practices which are the core of the teaching are known only to a few in the 'foreign branches'. My friend (whom I here call Izat Khan) had been as far as the Paghman Range of the Hindu-Kush mountains, and had been present at the meetings of the secret Sarmoon, but could tell me little about their secrets. Fifty or so years ago a party of *Yunanis* (this means 'Ionians') had been received by the Sheikh of the *Azimia* who lived in feudal splendour in Paghman; this was the only story of western contact with the Azimia.

I looked up Kafiristan in the best map I could find. The place was virtually unmapped. The latest available map was based upon reconnaissance surveys of 1878 and 1898. Try as I might, I could find no map which claimed to be the result of a geographical survey. Someone who should have known the facts told me that there was none such, even in Afghanistan itself. The U.S. Army Corps of Engineers' map seemed a mere copy of a Survey of India predecessor. The Indian part of the Survey was dated '1904-40'; and the Kafiristan portion of the area shown merely referred back to the '1878-98' reconnaissance. Kafiristan might almost not have existed. Though some glaciers and heights of the order of fourteen and twenty thousand feet were marked.

What about the people? And the language? My previous trips had started in a different way. At least one had had introductions for one stage of the journey. It was when I was pondering thus that I suddenly realised how very much early encouragement means. A little more travelling, more talking with people who knew Afghanistan, and I realised that I must have contacts if there were to be any real chance of success. In talks with Sufi mystics in Pakistan, India and other countries, I had come to realise one curious fact about the way in which they were thinking. In the first place, your average Sufi who was not a mere imitator of mystics was deeply concerned about humanity as a whole. Those who were higher up than the average in the invisible hierarchy seemed to share another basic bent of thought. This was that it was necessary for the Sufis, and the Sufis alone could do it, to bridge the gap between the developing cultures of the East and West. Since I had joined their ranks I too, had

a similar sensation. The reason seemed clear enough : there was
no other meeting-ground. All the co-operation in politics, in
education and economics, between the Orient and Occident, was
not bringing the two together at all. And deep down inside of
us, most people knew this. We had accepted that there was no
meeting-ground in religion : this had been established as early as
the time of the Crusades. That there was no deep co-operation
in material fields was clear to those who had seen the downfall
of one attempt after another to bridge the gap.

Nationalism and independence in the East had not brought
about widespread harmony between the former ruling countries
and the formerly ruled. People had claimed that the granting
of independence to the East would be a sort of panacea. All
would be well and cordial relations would be bound to return
when people were ruled by their own nationals. This had not
happened. In some cases the reverse had taken place.

In orthodox philosophy the East and West had taken leave of
one another centuries ago. There was no basic unity of ideas at
all, partly because, deep down, there was disharmony between
peoples of different cultures, different nations. We had diagnosed
the problem as due to one disease. When the remedy for the
diagnosed ailment was applied, the illness did not cease, was not
even ameliorated. The people who thought that the cure lay in
granting independence, economic help and so on refused to look
at the instances of the countries in which these measures had not
worked. Why? They were too busy looking for other countries
to grant independence to. They had no time to see whether they
were curing what they thought they were curing. I was no oppo-
nent of independence for anyone. But I could see that independence was not enough. As with many other things, the reforma-
tion had to start with the individual, had to start from within.
The materialists continued to reassure us and themselves that
'things would shake down', that as soon as the first wave of
patriotic fervour had passed, the East and the West would respect one another, and all would be well. But my travels and
talks with people at all levels showed me that people in the Asian
countries which had been independent for generations were still
not reconciled with the West. What did this mean?

It meant that the world was still waiting for a development
within humanity which would make humanity one, one body,

one heart. Plenty of people said that they had the answer. Nobody, as far as I could see, was applying it.

I had travelled and lived among the Sufis in Asia and Europe, in Africa and India. Sharing their lives and talking to them, becoming a member of their fraternities, I had found a group of people who were as worried about the future of the human race as I was. The difference between this group and those who talked a great deal about it in mass-communications media was, that the Sufis were trying to live that kind of life.

Their trusting me, as a member of another type of community was to them a practical expression of that actual living of human unity. None of them, I am sure, thought that I wanted to associate with them for cheap sensationalism: although they were strongly resistant to the approaches of Western occultists and even anthropologists. They got to know me, decided that I wanted to be like them, and accepted me, in an amazingly short space of time.

I took this matter up with Yunus, a friend who had been Abbot of a Sufi monastery in Iraq, and had now become a merchant in Pakistan. Did the Sufis as a whole want to project their message in the West as well as in the East? How did they think it would be done, if it were done? How could they avoid making themselves into just another 'cult' followed – for a time – by every crank intellectual and occultist at any given time or place?

Yunus understood me at once. 'Your answer is not as simple as it seems it might be. We can put a question, but we cannot always find the answer in a couple of words.

'You will find out, I think, if you spend more time among the Sufis, for you have to absorb their characteristic 'flavour'. Once you have been with the Sufis, really *of* the Sufis, you cannot believe that their Way will ever become degenerated as you describe.'

I flew from New Delhi to Karachi, through the usual kaleidoscope of air terminal, airport omnibus, boarding the aircraft, the flight, air terminal, and so on, almost in a daze. Asia has a way of giving you just what it wants to give. This form of transport seemed somehow from another world. I could not say that it was a Western way superimposed upon the East: not only because it was manned by Easterners, but because I had never, even in Europe, felt air travel to be a natural part of life.

As I sat strapped into my seat and crunched a peppermint, supposedly to keep my ears from 'popping', and looked around at the shining Sindhi faces of the businessman in every seat, I could not think that they belonged to any culture either.

CHAPTER SEVEN

Return to Kunji Zagh

The attempt to reach the Sufi centres of Kafiristan would have to wait until late Spring, whichever way I was travelling. This meant that I could spend some time at my parent monastery of Kunji Zagh; to learn more and to seek the reality behind Sufism from different angles. I made my way there, this time without my friend the Akhund (who was nowhere to be found), but by the same form of jolting motor-lorry 'bus' which now seemed, somehow, a more natural form of transport than any other. If a modern, air-conditioned desert omnibus such as they have in the Middle East had appeared, I am sure that I would have looked at it askance. But let nobody think that the East stays still. It compromises. Those who could travel by motor would generally do so, I noted, rather than going through the trouble of buying or hiring animals which would have to be fed and looked after. It was better to leave the worrying to the owner of the lorry.

The Murshid showed no surprise when I entered the building as though I belonged to it, though I think that he was glad to see me. From now on he addressed me as 'Haji' – pilgrim – although most of the other members of the community seemed to have been to Mecca, and were not styled by this honorific. This seemed to indicate that the Sufis felt my pilgrimage to have been something out of the ordinary, though they never said as much.

For the first few days of meditation and sharing the chores of the establishment I lost a great deal of the attitude towards life which clung to me while I was 'outside', or 'in the world'. Indeed, I could very easily have steeped myself in mystical practises and what must be considered introspection, had my teacher himself not repeatedly pulled me back to reality by talking about what could be considered to be mundane things. I did not at first realise that this was a part of the training. Before very long it became apparent that everything was a part of the training. The knack was to accept it as such, and not to allow the periods of self-awareness which were demanded to spread over one's whole mentality and merely substitute one form of 'conditioning' for another.

The Murshid encouraged us, then, to ask questions and often suggested them. Some of the implications of his remarks showed that he must be aware of the questionings in my mind: the re-assertion of decades of a certain brain-habit. This is the habit of trying to judge everything one sees, hears or thinks, and it is a characteristic of intellectuals in the East and West alike. Here is an example.

One morning when I had some free time I was looking at a very strange object which stood in lonely splendour on a wooden block. It was made of wood and upon it was nailed a piece of tin cut into an irregular shape. The wooden object reminded one more than anything else of a rough, primitive idol. Looking closer I saw that the wood was of a coarse-grained kind unfamiliar to me. On the ragged tin sheet there were several scratches, incised by some pointed instrument, which for me made no sense at all. By the side of the object, which stood about three feet high, was a bunch of dried grapes. I noted that the wood seemed to have been stained, or perhaps this was a result of some weathering. Three stones, rounded pebbles, were in a small cup beside the grapes. I looked at this unusual pheno-menon from every point of view. Could it be an idol, in a community which abhorred idols? Was there a message, some sort of composite meaning which could be derived from it through a proper intuitive understanding of symbols? Why had the grapes and the pebbles been placed there, and what did they signify?

When I returned to the *majlis* (session-room) my mind was almost wholly occupied by these thoughts and many others. There could have been a phallic symbolism to the object. Per-haps its meaning had been forgotten, and that it was reputed to have certain powers. It was of some importance, that was certain. Associations from wide reading in anthropology, psychology and history flooded into my mind. Patterns began to fit; theories were half-developing.

In this state of mind I sat on my small rug, not taking much notice of the other residents who were coming in and out, or merely sitting and meditating.

At about this point the Murshid came in, motioning me not to rise. Instead of taking his accustomed position, he came and half-knelt beside me. His weather-beaten face was relaxed, but his large eyes were twinkling.

'Have you see the *Be-asrar;* the thing which stands on the stone?' He obviously knew that I had, and that I was at that moment thinking about it. I nodded.

'Do you wonder what it is, why it is there? Or have you already decided?'

I told him that I was still wondering.

'It is there to make you think. It is there to make you try to fit it into some scheme of things. *It is there because it does not mean anything at all.* It is there to show you that you cannot relate everything to everything else just because you have a rupee's worth of reasoning faculty, one of the lowest faculties.'

The words were said in the kindest possible way, in spite of the reproach in them.

I suddenly realised what this meant, in a way which the mere academic acceptance of the facts would surely never have conveyed. I realised that if I had read of this experience in a book, and duly noted it as a good technique and a fine illustration of the limitations of thinking from a prejudiced point of view, it would never have been the same as going through the experience.

I said, 'Yes, you have demonstrated something which has been pointed out recently in the West. That is that for instance, patients treated by Freudian analysis have Freudian dreams, and those undergoing Jungian treatment have Jungian dreams.'

He must have read my mind. 'This may well be true. But do you think that this fact which you have just told me, which you have been told or have read somewhere, has the same life, the same reality about it, that there is to be found in the experience which you have just had?'

'No,' I told him, hurriedly, 'by no means. But I had to say something which approximated with the subject under discussion.'

'So you had to show me that you understood, that you followed what I said? Even though in doing so you were only invoking an approximation of the complete experience?'

'Yes, that is, I suppose, what it amounts to.'

'Then here is your lesson: when there is complete understanding, there is silence. There is no talk. If you share an experience with someone, and that is a true and real – I mean really deep – experience can you put it into words? Do you want to put it into words? When you are in love, does 'I love you' mean anything? Or is it the touch of a hand, the exchanging of a glance, which means real love?'

I had to admit that he was right.

'Something very important is happening in your mind when you have an experience' said the teacher. 'You take the experience in, and your mind labels it. To do this it has to split it up into a vast number of tiny impressions. Your mind may not be ready for the whole experience, so that the mind cannot handle the impressions. It will select some, and then transmit back to another part of your brain an assessment. This assessment is what intellectuals use. They deal in incomplete assessments. This is why some agree, some differ. In real experience there is no possibility of disagreement.'

This was by no means the only thing which happened at Kunji Zagh. The following day the Murshid sent for me and asked me to tell him what I thought about spiritual teachers. It was remarkable because this was a central point in my present thinking. I had realised that I was learning a great deal. Since my first Sufi contacts and activities, here in this very monastery of Kunji Zagh, I had found new dimensions to life. Apart from the interest and sympathy which I derived from my Sufi friends, I felt myself changed in a subtle way. This change, as far as the outside world was concerned, was largely material. This was to say, I realised as I took stock, I had developed abilities which I had not had before. They were of various kinds. In the first place, I did not lose my temper as before. Nobody had told me to try to restrain anger. But whereas I had in the past found that I was often angry when I was frustrated and annoyed, anger seemed to come now only in order to achieve some purpose. Again, on another level, my battle with the Arabic alphabet had been hard. I could read well enough but found great difficulty (as most Westerners do) in forming the letters in an elegant fashion. Most give up the effort: and a very considerable effort it is. To write like an Eastern calligrapher is an accomplishment which I had not really expected would ever be mine. Now, when I was making notes at lectures, I found that I had acquired this knack. This first came into my consciousness when I looked through a sheaf of notes and thought that they had been written by someone else. Then I saw that the material which I had just written was in the same even, neat, *Nastaliq* hand which dates from the classical period of Persian literature.

Other changes were too numerous to mention. Some of them were in my way of thinking, some in my reactions to what was said or heard, some seemed to be connected with an inner sense which sometimes seemed like conscience, sometimes like the feeling of achievement or confidence. But I realised that this sense was in some way the uniting of two or more normal sensations, combining to make them into one, into an instrument of some kind.

A great deal of this flashed into my mind when the Murshid asked me about spiritual teachers. I had been wondering how the Sufi Way corresponded in its results with other systems; and whether one could follow a different system and get the same results. This had brought up the whole question of the genuineness of the various ways of self-development. And here I, like most people, was stumped.

'There are as many Ways as there are souls of men' said the Murshid, while he was waiting for me to reply.

I asked him who were the real teachers, and how one could tell who was a real teacher.

'A sugar-loaf you weigh against a weight, or against another sugar-loaf' he said, with a laugh. 'A teacher you cannot weigh against another teacher. You have to weigh him against yourself. Now comes your problem : when you are weighing a teacher you are not weighing an inert thing. He can, if he desires, increase or decrease his weight. Do you understand me?'

'Do you mean that the teacher has to accept me before I can judge him?'

'It is something as difficult as that. You see, you cannot choose your teacher by logic. The reason is that logic does not extend into the field in which the teacher is operating. This is why it is better for the teacher to choose you.'

'But if logic is not enough, surely the "unripe" will not be able to recognise the teacher? Can the teacher come up to him and say : "I am your teacher?" And if he does, the student cannot tell whether he is the real teacher or not.'

'This is why' said the Murshid, 'the so-called "choice" of a teacher is not a choice at all. What happens is this. The would-be disciple approaches the potential teacher and opens his heart to him. This means that he allows himself to become receptive to what the teacher is *saying and doing*. He must absorb something of the whole entity, the wholeness, the personage of the teacher *and his works*. Then a contact can be made. There is a recognition in the mind of the disciple that this is the teacher for him. If the recognition is false, the teacher will send him packing.'

'And if the teacher is false, and either thinks that a real recognition has taken place?' I asked.

'In that case you have the formation of groups fanatically attached to the personality of a teacher, trying to justify him in every way, and talking about his miracles. These are false and also useful but incomplete schools. This is the stage at which many ascetics have stopped.'

'Then how does the disciple know when he is following a true teacher?'

'Because something has happened to him, inside. This something is reflected in everything which he does. He is not the same man after the regeneration is accomplished. The change in the social powers and the material achievements of the disciple are obvious to everyone : obvious to the complete outsider, who always remarks upon it. A man is attracted to a teacher of the degree of sincerity which he has himself attained.'

'You mean that people say "How different you are! How you have changed"?'

'Much more than that. People start to *feel* some sort of power emanating from you. Further, you progress in the material world to such an extent that new faculties enable you to prevail over ordinary people. This, naturally enough, brings such things as possessions, money, promotion, happiness. Many of these things are very, very obvious to the uninitiated.'

'So you must keep in touch with the world, partly in order to see that yardstick working – the effect which you have upon the uninitiated?'

'Yes. This is one reason why false teachers often spend all of their time "out of the world". There is nobody to say that their disciples have not progressed as human beings.'

'But not all those schools which are not Sufi ones claim to regenerate man so that he shall become successful materially.'

'This is precisely the absurdity of the schools. Man is born human, and *all* his potentialities are to be used. Otherwise life is a mockery. To turn him into an imitation of a totally spiritual being is either attempted fraud or else (more likely) a misunderstanding of asceticism.'

'Can asceticism take place in the midst of society?'

'Yes, of course it can. There is a function in temporary withdrawal for the purposes of certain parts of the work, but total withdrawal is nonsense.'

'What about the Yogis with withered arms held above their heads?'

'You cannot generalise, and we do not use theoretical cases. Meet one, and your inner sense will tell you. I will now tell you about some that I have met, out of many. In some, you can tell that they are merely signposts. The withered arm is a sign of the death-potential of the body. The man on a bed of spikes may be a fraud. He may, on the other hand, have been placed there by a teacher who wants to show something to the public, to prepare them for a lesson. The Sufis are opposed, of course, to such abominations. The drawback of too many Yogic practises is that they are partial and often carried out at the behest of teachers who are only *trying to perfect a system*. This means that the individual is sacrificed to the group.'

'How did the Sufis find out their secrets, then, if one way is by experimentation?'

'By balancing the physical with the mental, and by a form of intuition. That is all I can say. It is a harmony with creation. How does a shepherd know when to collect his flock because a storm threatens? Sometimes by assessment, sometimes by experience.'

'So Sufism stands or falls on its record of success?'

'Sufism does not stand or fall: it exists. People who are brought up in Sufism excel; so do people who join it later in life. But people brought up on Yoga, say, in most forms, merely become Yogis; they do not become more distinguished or valuable to the world. People who join Yoga after they have established themselves in the world are no advertisement for Yoga.'

'And yet the original teaching was the same?'

'Not *was,* but *is.* The original teaching is always there. We hold on to it and have not gone out of contact with it. These other cults have it, but they do not realise that they must have theory and practice, be in the world and not of the world, that they must combine, combine. The Sufi has to weave from his experience a fine net in which he catches the *baraka,* the Sufi essence. Then he becomes enlightened. The others carry on with half a weapon, hoping to conquer with it. Unbalanced development is bound to produce something lopsided. Lopsided people are sure to crowd around lopsided beliefs. The ordinary man comes to the Sufi: and he becomes an extraordinary man.'

'But this man has to have a certain something which enables him to accept the Sufis. The presence of that spark is what we call a blessing.'

Munawwar Husain, a tall, rather shy member of the fraternity, originating from the Persian Caspian area, became a special friend of mine. We walked together under the mulberry trees, shared kitchen tasks, arrived at a sort of understanding which, in a Western atmosphere I would have called friendship. But I was sure that he knew something that I did not, and that he wanted to communicate it to me. In a Western atmosphere I would have tackled him about it, asked him whether he was being evasive when I put questions to him, whether there was some reservation about me. Perhaps, I thought, the barrier between the European and the Oriental was too great; somewhere inside of him he thinks of me as an infidel. After all, we had not shared a way of life, his forebears and I, since the middle ages.

One day, when I had decided to try to penetrate this barrier between us, something anticipated me. Munawwar and I were sitting on the bank of a foaming brook, repeating together the chant of the Order, when he turned his large eyes towards me, and said in his singsong Persian voice: 'Brother, if I reproach you, it is because I have a friendship for you and therefore for all of yours which I cannot any longer suppress.'

I looked at him without being able to utter a word.

He went on: 'You repeat the Zikr with feeling, with such feeling that it rings to me like the enthusiasm of one who feels in it a magical chant. This, you say as you say the words of the invocation, is the thing which will bring me to God, to Truth, to Love, to whatever you feel you need. Am I right?'

I said: 'You may be right, but that is, surely, a measure of my aspiration. I do seek truth. I do believe, sincerely, that you here have something which we in the West may have lost. I desire only to bring myself into harmony with it.'

He bowed his head. 'If I can communicate to you, my dear friend, how we think of one another and about our holy task, you may understand that you must divorce your desire and your aspiration. That way lies truth.'

I told him that I did not understand. 'No. What I mean is that you are looking for a formula which will lead you to truth. You are anxious to get into the inner ring. You pause beside the library, where you think there may be books which will tell you secrets. You hope for transformation by getting "something we have" which you think you yourself have not got. That is the difference between the East and the West. It has nothing to do with your education or the religion of your fathers, or whether we think that you are an infidel or not.'

These last words, which so clearly echoed my feelings about his possible attitude towards me, magnetized my attention. I was in no doubt that he had directly read my mind.

'At Kunji Zagh,' he said, 'we have people who are nominally Christians, fire-worshippers, Hindus, freethinkers. What do you think holds us together? Is it the *baraka* of this place? Is it greed for secrets? No, it is the consciousness of the holy. You are still desiring easy secrets. Please believe me when I tell you that this is the last way in which you will receive them.'

I had never heard him talk like this before, and my emotions were powerfully stirred. I asked him to give me a piece of advice, any corrective for the way in which I thought, if he could give me one.

'Yes. Learn. Do not criticise. Do not believe. Acquire knowledge of the attitude towards these great and secret things which we call the Teaching. And ask Sufi Abdul-Hamid about what happened to the Russian Tatar.'

This was the first I had heard of the mystic and enigmatic figure who had become famous in Europe and America as the teacher of a new 'system', the controversial G. I. Gurdjieff.

One day, sitting with a group of the Sufis at Kunji Zagh, I saw a newcomer; an Arab-looking dervish, quite young and with the air of indifference that comes so soon to those who spend their time in isolated places – unless they have something to do. I went over to him, and asked him where he came from. At least I could exercise my Arabic a little, and there was now time every evening after our studies, as the pace had slackened off a little.

He was from Iraq, from near Baghdad, and he had been to see the *Khwaja al-Ajami* (the Eastern Master) in Damascus. They say that if you stay at one point long enough, what you are seeking will always come past. In my case this had been for some time, this very Eastern Master. He was the Studious King, the man I most wanted to meet, though I had not dared to say so to the head of the monastery; for such sentiments were discouraged. One does not, in Sufi circles, agitate to be sent somewhere just because one feels like it, however strongly. This is a matter for the superior, the teacher. But until now I had no idea where the Shah might be found. Now there was hope that he might come here.

As we were eating our evening meal, the Murshid made a sign to me afterwards; and I followed him to his study. 'You are to go to *Damishq;*' he said. 'You will find Tarzizada, and you will stay with him. When you have finished there you may resume your journey to Muristan. This should be in three or four months' time. Return via this *Khanqa,* and be prepared to go into Afghanistan. You will spend some time with the people of the Hindu Kush, and then travel to the East, towards the Pamirs and Badakhshan.'

I knew that I was headed for a meeting with the man about whom all the Sufis were interested, and whose precise mission only the Murshids knew, it was said that he would travel to the West in the end, but I did not know that I would meet him there, or what the West meant : for sometimes it means Morocco or Algeria, and sometimes Europe. 'West', as used in Central Asia, could easily mean Syria as well, and I was off to Syria : via Herat, Persia and Iraq. I decided to visit a little-known Christian community en route.

CHAPTER EIGHT

The Followers of Jesus

The followers of Isa, son of Maryam – Jesus the son of Mary – generally call themselves Moslems and inhabit a number of villages scattered throughout the Western area of Afghanistan whose centre is Herat. I had heard of them several times, but considered that they were probably people who had been converted by European missionaries from Eastern Persia, or else that they were a relic of the times when Herat had been a flourishing bishopric of the Nestorian rite, before the Arabs conquered Persia in the seventh and eight centuries.

But, from their own accounts and what I could observe, they seem to come from some much older source.

I found them through one of the deputies of the Mir of Gazarga, the descendant of Mohammed under whose protection they are. Gazarga is the shrine where Abdullah Ansar, a Sufi mystic and great local saint, is buried in a magnificent tomb formerly much visited by the emperors of India and other notables.

There must be about a thousand of these Christians. Their chief is the Abba Yahiyya (Father John), who can recite the succession of teachers through nearly sixty generations to – Isa, son of Mary, of 'nazara', the Kashmiri.

According to these People, Jesus escaped from the Cross, was hidden by friends, was helped to flee to India, where he had been before during his youth, and settled in Kashmir, where he is revered as an ancient teacher, Yuz Asaf. It is from this period of the supposed life of Jesus that these people claim to have got their message.

I had several conversations with the Abba; though, not unnaturally if his story was true, there were few points on Christian doctrine as we know it today that we could recognise.

The Abba lived on a farm, and like all the 'Christians' says that their teacher stipulated that his followers should always have a worldly vocation. Jesus, according to this community, was a carpenter and also a shepherd. He had the power to perform miracles, and he did indeed 'die for the sake of his people'. This death, astonishingly enough, is not the death generally assumed. The death was a real one, but it took place long before Jesus started his mission, and it was as a result of this experience that he met God and was sent back to mankind to warn them of their possible fate if they did not seek love and truth.

The 'Traditions of the Masih' (anointed one) is the holy book of the community. They do not believe in the New Testament; or, rather, they say that these Traditions are the New Testament, and that the Gospels which we have are partly true but generally written by people who did not understand the teachings of the Master.

Abba Yahiyya, a towering figure with the face of a saint, was certainly an erudite man, and he knew his own scriptures, plus a great deal of the Jewish writings, very well indeed. He had heard of the teachings of the 'heretics' as he called what we would call the various sects of Christians known to us; and he wanted no part of them.

'My son,' he said, in his softly accented Persian, 'these people are reading and repeating a part of the story. They have completely misunderstood the message. We have the story told us by the Master, and through Him we will be saved and made whole. Some of the events in that document which you call the Bible are true, but a great deal is made up or imagined or put in for less than worthy reasons. Isa lived for over thirty years after the materials you have were completed, and He told us what was true.'

Briefly, the doctrine is that Jesus was the Son of God because He had attained that rank through his goodness and sacrifices. Thus He was equal to a divine person. He came after John the Baptist, who himself had reached the highest degree of development possible at that time. John baptised with water, Jesus with spirit and fire. These were the three stages of understanding, which were taught by our Christians.

There was a great deal of confusion at first, because I was talking about sacraments and being saved, while it took me some time to realise that Abba John's people regarded baptism, the Holy Ghost and the Kingdom of God to be three stages in a system of human illumination. This is what they claim is the function of the Church : the preservation of and administration of these three 'developments' for the worshipers.

There is a ritual meal, like the Last Supper, but this is carried out once a week. Bread and wine are eaten, but as symbolic of the grosser and finer nutritions which are the experiences of attainment of nearness to God.

While it is possible to consider these people as mere heretics, or else as followers of someone else who impersonated Jesus, yet I was singularly impressed by their piety, their feeling of certainty, their simplicity and lack of the unpleasant forms of fervour which one often finds in minority cults. They were convinced, too, that the day would come when the world would discover the truth about Jesus. When this took place, it would be the mission of the Followers to come out into the open and teach those who wanted to believe in Jesus the methods by which a man or woman could 'enter the Kingdom'.

Sufi Abdul-Hamid Khan, Master of the Royal Afghan Mint and something of a polymath – military engineer, calligraphist, sage and expert on rhythmic exercises – must have been over ninety years of age. A follower of the Mir of Gazarga, he could remember in considerable detail the events which had taken place eighty or more years ago.

A frequent visitor to Kunji Zagh, he had spent many years in Bokhara, and it was there that he had come across the redoubtable Gurdjieff, whose studies of Eastern metaphysical systems were introduced into Europe about the time of the First World War.

Although the people of Kunji Zagh called Gurdjieff 'The Russian Tatar', Sufi Abdul-Hamid said that he was in reality partly Mongolian, part-Russian, part-Greek. According to the Sufi, this Jurjizada (Son of George) had once been a Theosophist, had also studied in an Orthodox seminary, and 'was responsive' to the Sufic 'waves' – could, in other words, contact the mental activity which emanated from the 'work' of the dervishes. This, together with a curiosity about the occult, led him to the shrine of Bahauddin, the Naqshbandi teacher in Bokhara.

Here another Bahauddin, known as Dervish Baha, had taught him certain 'secrets'. Among them were the 'sacred dances' or movements made by the dervishes, the rules of the Order and the 'inner interpretation' of the Sufi texts. Then he sent him on a tour of the centres of the Sufis, some in Egypt, some in Syria, some in India.

Seeing the strange effects of the Sufi practices, Gurdjieff decided that he would find out how they worked. In order to do this, he and a number of friends collected as much of the material used by the Order as they could, and fled with it 'to the West'.

Unfortunately, continued Abdul-Hamid, Jurjizada was at too early a stage to do anything final with the material. He had not yet learned, for instance, that the exercises and the music had to be carried out with special people at certain times in a special order of events. As a result he propounded the theory of the Complete Man without being able to take it into practice.

Further, Gurdjieff tried to make the method work by trying out the exercises on a large number of people. The result?

'Here in Afghanistan we still receive, like faint radio messages, the influence of the minds of the pupils of Gurdjieff, coming from far away. They must still be carrying on the exercises, but they don't know how, when or with whom to do them.'

As soon as I got back to Europe, I found that some at least of this information might be true. After the first War, the Russian and a disciple of his, the philosopher Ouspensky, settled in France and England respectively. They set up teaching groups, and – I was told – several of these still existed. But they remained fully secret. Probably, like the custodians of any secret knowledge which had become reduced in quality, they would continue to operate, perhaps for generations.

The 'Followers of Jesus' carried out a ring-dance which they said was originally the method of worship of the early Christians but had been dropped because nobody now knew how to select the various 'congregations' which could carry it out successfully. It seemed that, in company with the dervishes, these people believed that it was not enough to worship together. What really counted was who worshipped with whom, when and where. It was easy to see that such a complicated ritual would have little chance of persisting in a widespread community, where the priest officiating would, by logic, be compelled to carry out numerous services: one for each 'circle' of people who were mutually attuned in worship.

I had a glorious time in Herat; for life in Afghanistan can be as close to paradise as anything one could imagine. One of the Herati elders, chiefs of lands and villages, took me shooting, to bring back wild duck and large delicious partridges from the meadows of his estates. We sat in the great reception-hall of the castle of Aramabad – the Abode of Bliss – and listened to tales of love and war, of the mystique of making spiced rice *pilau,* of the lost treasure of the loot of Delhi. This was buried, according to local tradition, near Herat by Ahmad Shah, the general of Nadir the Persian, instead of returning it to his royal employer in Persia in the eighteenth century.

We played the game of 'I remember', a sort of psychological-cum-training game devised, it was said, by the Sufis to amuse and instruct the people of Khorasan. Several 'experts' on Europe, some of whom had never been farther away than Kabul, were collected by the Sardar and asked to converse with me. They were in a ticklish situation, because they had dined out on their stories of the West for so long that they were word-perfect in their invented or half-understood tales. And the audience was word-perfect, too. This meant that unless I agreed with them and confirmed every particular, *I* would be considered some sort of fraud.

These 'experts' were a schoolmaster, a man who had been in the service of an Afghan chief who was reputed to have been in France but in reality spent most of his free time in Beirut, and a number of former students, who had read a lot of Western books without the formality of getting a grounding in English, French, German, or whatever it was, to enable them to understand exactly what they said.

Eventually, with the help of an Afghan merchant of rugs and textiles, I set out for Islam Qilla, the frontier post for Persia. It was a hard and tiresome journey, with the dust from the road often swathing the little Minibus in which we travelled.

When we got to Islam Qilla the frontier guards offered us tea and boiled eggs and refused to let me through.

They were, like all Afghan soldiers, tough and fearsome-looking, enormously polite and evidently trained to a hair. They looked like cleaned-up brigands. No, I could not go through. **My passport was not in order. I had no entry visa for Afghanis-**

tan. Therefore I was not here at all. If I was not here, I could not very well leave . . .

Nobody, even the immigration officer, seemed to mind that I had entered Afghanistan, it seemed, illegally. There was no question of investigating, or holding me. But I could not leave.

While we were trying to reason with the guards, fate intervened. An enormous streamlined shooting-brake, caked with dust, came roaring down the Herat road and came to a screeching stop just in front of our vehicle. A massive, hatchet-faced figure with a shaggy sheepskin cap and riding boots over his mohair suit, climbed out. He waved to the guards to let him through. I imagined that he was the Governor of a province, at least, as they say in Afghanistan.

While his passport was being stamped, not without alacrity, this apparition, baring his teeth in an almost over-charming smile, said : 'Iran miri?' (art thou going to Persia?) I said that I was, but that they would not let me through. His brow darkened. 'Not let you through? What have you done?'

'Ya Shaghali hakim-i-a'la, O High-Ranking Governor,' I said, 'I am a poor traveller . . .'

'Yes, yes,' he interrupted brusquely, 'but whose guest are you?'

'Well, I have been the guest of the Mir of Gazar Gah . . .'

'Gazar Gah!' he roared, turning back to the officials with such speed that he collided with one, who fell to the ground, 'O sons of burnt fathers, are you stopping this guest of ours from going on his way?'

Someone murmered that my passport was not in order.

'Passport? Passport? Am *I* not better than any passport?'

It seemed more than a mere rhetorical statement, for the man seemed to wait for a reply.

'*Bali saheb*' – Yes, Sir.

'Now wait a minute, my friend. Be aware of what I am saying. What are you people? You are servants of Afghanistan. What is Afghanistan? It is the country which exists only because of the existence of the Prophet. Who is the Wali of Gazargah? He is one of the People of the House, of the family of the Prophet. Peace and the blessings of Allah upon him.'

He glared around him, while all dutifully echoed his last sentence.

Then he nodded. 'Then it is all settled. We may have democracy in this country now, but by God we will not have any of that Persian nonsense about making trouble for our friends. What are you? You are *Government officials*. That means, "Servants of the people and their guests." It does *not* mean "Runts recruited from the cesspits of Kabul and stained with ink, slithering among heaps of papers". Do you understand?'

They understood.

'Thanks to God – may His name be Exalted – no piece of paper in this country can yet prevent people like me (he thumped his chest) from trickling the blood of dogs upon the ground. Do you understand that?'

They understood.

'Let them go then.'

He turned to me. 'I am a disciple of the Saints, through the kindness of the Deity' he said.

He stayed with us until we had got a Persian visa issued, by a mixture of reproaches and accusations, all manufactured by our new friend. By the time the terrified Persians were allowed to enter their control hut, they were under the impression that it was their fault, in some way, that I had not had a visa at the start.

As he waved goodbye, the driver of the station-wagon said to me, 'And another thing. I don't like traders like your friend. Tell him to be an honest man, because I have memorised his face.'

And he was off.

CHAPTER NINE

Damascus

Perhaps more than any other Arab land, Syria contains in full measure that elusive atmosphere of strangeness and intimacy which literally fascinates the foreigner. Wander down the Great Souk of Damascus any day of the week, and you will see foreign tourists gazing at the passing scene, at a striding beduin sheikh or a damascened blade, with all the intense abstraction that the East can draw down. And Damascus is the heart of Syria, perhaps of the present-day Arab soul.

While Jeddah is mostly modern, stark and matter-of-fact, Mecca soulful, Cairo neither one thing nor another, Damascus gleams and then hides herself, like the gem she is, redolent of the agelessness of a place believed to be the oldest inhabited city on earth. Damascus is mentioned in Genesis (Chapter xiv); holds the Church of St. John the Baptist; became the headquarters of the hosts of Saladin, and has been the capital of a Saracen world empire, that of the Sons of Omeyya, almost thirteen hundred years ago.

Syria, unlike most Middle Eastern lands, is fertile and under-populated. The fruits and flowers of a smiling country fill her bazaars. Stern-browe᷄, silent Druses from the mountains pace her streets, and Roman remains can still be seen in the Street Called Straight: which is still called The Straight Street. In the year 1440, Damascus was devastated by Tamerlane. All these facts, these impressions, crowd into the mind as one joins in the jostling throng which makes up today's Damascus: once a part of the ancient Egyptian Empire and – when I was there – newly freed from the clutches of a second Nilotic despot.

All over the world, from Los Angeles to Tokyo, from Ghana to remote Pacific Islands, Syrian traders send their profits home; and help to enrich their homeland further with today's treasure, foreign exchange. Like its history, Syria's people are stratified: the workers, the peasants, the sheikhs and their subjects; the feudal aristocrats and the traders. Like the regimes before them, they vary much in quality and in popularity.

Khalid, son of Tarzi ('The Tailor') was named after the first Arab conqueror of Syria; and he was my first Syrian Sufi friend. Khalid took me to his immense mansion within the city, whose towering walls hid a house the like of which there are many in Damascus. As in Spain, Morocco and other places where Arab influence has been architecturally strong, the house was meant for living in, not for looking at. As a result the outer walls were utterly plain, the doors solid but uninteresting. Once within, however, the resources of a mediaeval caliph seemed at our disposal. Sudanese servants, a fountain playing in a lapis-lazuli bowl, ceilings embellished with gold-leaf and calligraphic writing – a carp fashioned from a single huge piece of rock-crystal ('brought from China in the ninth century') : this was the home of an Arabian-Nights character.

In the central courtyard, something like a Hispano-Moorish patio, I found the group of people which always seems inseparable from Middle Eastern life. Visitors from afar, with some sort of introduction to the master of the house; friends of the adolescent children, a teacher or two, a religious devotee, a doctor of law. They sat and talked, waiting to see the host, or having come here merely to exchange information, or perhaps to 'make a visit', which is a way of passing the time. It was a relief to get away from the too-sharp Eastern and Western impacts which seemed to struggle in the open in Damascus town. The vestiges of French culture and the upthrusting intellectualism of the *effendi* who had forsaken his culture and wore his modernity without grace. The things that foreigners prize in Syria, as in so many other Oriental countries, are often the things that the vocal townspeople are trying to live down. And nobody is ever rude enough to tell the Westernised Easterner that, as often as not, he is a very sorry copy of an European, no matter how much money he has spent upon the attempted transformation.

In a home like Khalid's you can generally assess the nature and quality of the host by his guests. Sometimes it will be a courtyard filled with argumentative university students, spouting the memorised arguments of political theorists; sometimes a mass of grave-faced divines in robes and turbans deliberating some nice point of theology where deadlock had already been reached a thousand years and more ago. At least six of these were not Syrians, not even Arabs. Their presence probably influenced the atmosphere more than one realised. Arabic, French, and English were being spoken.

Khalid had wandered off to have a session with some kind of land agent, and I found myself sitting on a leather-covered low bench with some of the foreigners. 'I like this habit of letting your guests entertain each other' said an earnest young American to me, as soon as I sat down, 'Who are you?' There is, of course, no genuine answer to such a question. In order not to introduce any note of disharmony into the proceedings, I told him that I travelled in diesel-trucks : which I often did. 'Yeah?' he said, 'find them hard to sell?'

'Not too hard to sell' I said. This was true enough, because I had never tried to sell them, anyway. The technique which I was automatically using, that of playing upon words in order to illustrate their shortcomings, was lost upon him. It was used by the ancient Greek teachers, and has now deteriorated into a clash of wits in modern philosophy. The Sufis still use it, often in their stride. Comedians use it to wring a joke out of the contradictions found in phrases. The Irish seem to use it as a matter of course.

As generally happens when one joins a group of people, I was soon assimilated into the crowd; and they carried on talking without paying much attention to me. It was about the middle of the afternoon, and it looked as though the discussion had been going on for some time. Or perhaps they came here every day, to mingle in a clublike atmosphere.

The reason for the assembly here, or rather for this assembly being composed of these particular people, was less due to the personality of the host than to that of one of his guests. This guest, as I already knew, was the comparatively young man variously called *Shargharb* (a composite word, made up out of the Arabic words East and West); *Shariq* – the Illuminator; or, merely, *Shah* (king). He was, in fact, the person whom I had been seeking for a very long time; the same whom the community at Kunji Zagh called the Studious King : a direct translation of his name : more completely rendered as 'The Presence, Idries Shah, the Hashimite'. He was the man whose name I had first heard at Kunji Zagh.

The American now started to tell a story about this personage. 'I first met this guy in Cairo see? When I had had a couple of talks with him he asked me to go to see him in a room he had near the Azhar University. The place was crowded with students and all kinds. When I got there, first strange thing happened was somebody told him a certain old man was ill. He said, "I must go to him." This other fellow said, "He won't allow you to heal him, because he does not believe in it." But he had stood up and was winding a scarf around his neck – it was Winter, see?

'As we walked out of the building he said to me "They can't take away from me the merit of visiting the sick, because there is something for me in it. This is the way to tell them, not to say that you are going to do anything *for* them. What's the difference anyway?"'

'So eventually after a long walk we arrive at a small house where a Copt is living. His wife opens the door and this old man is lying in a very comfortable bed. He is a shopkeeper and quite well heeled, I would say. He seems to be about seventy years old. There are about ten of us in the group, and we can hardly get into the room, because it is so small. But nobody tries to stop us, it is all quite neighbourly. When the Copt sees this man, he groans and closes his eyes. Then our man raises his hands above the face of the Copt, and we wait for him to say something. But he doesn't say anything. He smiles and takes the oldster's hand.

'Then he just says, *"Tawab"*, which means a kind of merit for visiting the sick and poor, you know. Then he leaves the house, after asking the old woman how she is. She says she's got rheumatism but that the priest is coming and that will comfort everyone. Her maid has broken her leg, but it should mend all right.'

The American seems anxious for us to absorb all the details he can give.

'I ask our man what was wrong with the Copt. He does not know, and asks one of his friends, the one who came with the news. It is heart trouble and several other things wrong inside, he says. The man cannot live, and he is in pain. He just smiles and says, "we do all we can". That is sufficient to us. When we gain *tawab* so does everyone else, to a greater or lesser degree.'

The American stopped and looked into the distance. 'What happened then?' I asked him.

'O yeah. Then, I heard that he had been three times to see this old guy. The old guy was better and up on his feet. The maid was better, and cheerful. And the wife had no rheumatism.'

'That was all either to be expected, or it was the effect of suggestion' said a quiet but dignified-looking man of about fifty who was listening. He was very well dressed in a Western suit and looked as if he might have been a lawyer.

'Yeah, yeah,' said the American, 'you believe what you want to believe. It will do you more good.'

'I think you are a sensation-seeker' said the other, in his calm, careful way, his English a little rusty, perhaps, from infrequent use.

'Then what about me?' rejoined the American. 'I did not believe in him, did not even ask him to help me; but he sure cured my asthma.'

'It is the asthma of the mind' said the middle-aged man, 'and the imagination puts away what it creates.'

A little, wiry and excitable figure whom the others had addressed as Hatim and who had been sitting on the floor now stood up. 'You talk about medical treatment. He helped me more than that. If I am sick I go to a doctor. But if I am poor, and a man makes me a success, what about that?'

We all looked at him. He did not look like a success. What kind of success was he? We were soon to be informed. 'I tell you in a short time' said Hatim.

Telescoping the story, it seems that Hatim was a Persian. He met the teacher one day on a lonely road, and was given a lift in a car by him. The Sufi asked him what he wanted from life. 'I want square meals and a fair chance' was what he felt himself impelled to say. 'Very well,' said the "king", 'all you have to do is to sit at such-and-such a cafe, between certain hours, and you will gain your desire.'

Hatim went to the cafe in Baghdad (which was their destination) and wondered how his destiny would be fulfilled. He was a mechanic, quite handy with machines of all kinds. After he had been in the cafe for less than half an hour a man came up, sat at his table, offered him a job servicing motor-vehicles which he owned, and paid the fees for him to enter a language school.

Had Hatim told the Shah that he was a mechanic? 'Of course not. Anyway, he does not know my employer – you can check on it.'

I asked him what he was doing in Syria, if he was a mechanic employed in Iraq. 'I have come to kiss his feet, that is what.'

'Have you seen him since you got your job?' I asked Hatim. 'Yes,' he said, 'and I asked him how he got his powers and how they work. Do you know what he told me? He just said: "You are a good mechanic, Hatim Jan. You repair an engine for a man who does not understand anything about motors. He asks you how exactly you did it, and how it works. What do you tell him?" Of course he was right. If it *is* something like that, you can't explain, can you?'

'Nothing can be done without the Will of Allah, the All-Powerful,' said one of the ancients who had placed himself near us and had had the gist of the conversation translated for him by another member of the group. 'The man – may he be long of days – has the blessings of Allah and the Prophet – Peace upon Him and his Family – because he is descended from the House of Hashim.'

Now he went into a long description of the miracles performed by the members of the House of the Prophet. There was a tradition that every lineal descendant of Mohammed had two gifts: one was the *baraka,* blessing, which enabled him to do good even when it appeared to be evil. The second was the secret training-system which made the Sharifs, the descendents, into superior people. Some said that this was the inner teaching of the way of the Sufis. There was no doubt that almost all the Sufi orders traced their spiritual pedigree from the Prophet Mohammed. He gave examples of great Sufis of the Hashimite family. The theory of this hidden merit in this line had been misused more than once in the past. People claiming to be descendants of the Prophet had organised such bodies as the Assassins, which later became a terrorist society which threatened the peace of the Middle East for many years. But this Shah was known to belong to one of the oldest and most outstanding branches of the family tree.

I had heard it said before that the Sufi teaching was the inner teaching of Mohammed, reserved for a few disciples, of whom Ali, his son-in-law was one. All Sharifs are descended from Ali, who was Mohammed's cousin as well as the husband of Fatima, his daughter. 'But surely,' I said, 'the Sufis themselves claim that the teaching is far older than the House of the Prophet? There are traces of it in many countries, and in writings which date from before Mohammed.'

'I merely report what is said,' replied the ancient, 'and I know that the Sufis claim that only in the Prophetic House was this learning preserved until it was again given out to all after the conquests of Islam all over the East. I myself am a theologian and doctor of Islamic Law. I am not a Sufi, but I respect the great Sufis because of those of them who were legal masters. One was Ghazzali, another was Imam abu Hanifa.'

The conversation became general again. 'Talking of families' said an Indian, 'I know something about the father of this Sufi of ours. I saw his father storm at a certain man who wanted to get to England. The man stayed behind, but his companion went. The companion caught smallpox on the way and died.'

'That could have been a coincidence' said the middle-aged man.

'And how many times does a coincidence have to happen before it is not a coincidence and becomes a fact?' asked the Indian, who I was to discover had a real taste for disputation. 'You attach a battery to wires and then a lamp to the other end You get a light. This is a coincidence, because it is the co-happening of certain things. But it is also a fact.'

'Ah,' said the middle-aged man, triumphantly, 'but you can't get your Sufi to repeat every miracle of his in that way, so they are not facts.'

'Nobody has ever repeated a miracle to order, just because someone told him to do so,' said the Indian, 'I have myself seen one Hindu sadhu walking on water, because he wanted to cross a river. If I had asked him to do it again he would not. Why should he? Miracles are for a purpose, not for a demonstration. They are therefore more practical than scientific demonstrations.'

Our host had joined us, and smiled reflectively as he interrupted. 'A young man here came to see our Sayyed Sufi when he was here last. He asked for help in his examinations. The Sayyed said that he would have to consult his inner self.' After a moment's reflection he held his hands above the boy's head. Then he sent him away, without another word. The boy passed his examinations. And there was another occasion. The postman brought in a letter, and before he had read it he just turned to me and said "Please prepare another bed for a friend". The letter announced the arrival of someone who wanted to see him. These may have been coincidence. Or they may have been deliberate deception.

'One day he said to me, "Khalid, beware of the man with hennaed hair", and the same day someone with dyed hair whom I had trusted tried to deceive me over a business matter. When he went to Paris he wrote to me, saying that he thought that I should buy some land if I felt like it, as some would be offered me. I bought it when the offer came, and it has now been re-sold at a profit of over ten times, for building. All these things may be deception, or self-deception, but I am content, because the fact remains that I am better off, and I have him as a friend.'

'Don't you see' said the middle-aged man irritably, 'that all this is a matter of prestige? A person with enough prestige can make people believe anything.'

'But there wasn't any prestige in the land business,' said Khalid.

The other man ignored him. 'You just look for signs of the unknown, because it thrills you. You seek the unknown and then magnify it.'

'Like his curing my stiff arm, and with one long glance giving a new life, new hope, to a young woman who was in a mental condition?' Khalid was not exactly ruffled, but he was undoubtedly convinced that he was right.

'Like looking for anything that you can magnify, without realising it.'

'I look for it, because I believe that it is there. I believe that this is the only thing which can explain so-called miracles. But if I were to magnify it, I would lose by it. If you allow your emotions to rule you, you will lose touch with the world, and you will not be able to see the truth. This is perhaps what is happening to you. I dare not follow this man from sheer curiosity. If I did, he would cast me off. I have seen it done. Believe me, this kind of person does not appear often, perhaps once in a generation. There was one in my father's time, and there is another here, in this building, now, and you feel that it cannot be true because you cannot measure it.'

Over in one corner, sitting on a large leather-covered cushion and closely attended by several young men of military aspect was a distinguished-looking man in his sixties. He was short and volatile, and as I went across to the group I heard him addressed as 'Excellency'.

'Meet the Pasha,' said the engineer.

I realised with some surprise that I was now shaking hands with an illustrious Middle Eastern statesman.

What was he doing here? he smiled. 'You are evidently a stranger to the gatherings of dervishes, my friend' he said, 'you should know that we travel when and where we wish, and we associate with whom we wish. Only in this way can our work be done.'

He asked me many questions about myself, always in a low voice, in almost perfectly accented English. I realised that here was a man to be reckoned with. His distinguished career which had grown from small beginnings was due to some magic, some capacity, which is not often seen in the ordinary man.

I asked the Pasha whether his being a dervish had contributed towards his worldly success. He seemed highly amused. 'Oh, yes, of course, you Westerners are always looking for the cause of something – the magic spell which will explain a man's success or failure. But in this case you are right. I *do* nothing, but I am a fakir.' Since fakirs are nicknamed the Howling Dervishes, and most accounts of them include hair-raising stories of bands of dishevelled semi-beggars shouting in the streets, I was a little taken aback. And I said so. He silenced me with one of his quick gestures. 'Brother, remember the proverb: "The donkey judges all delights by the quality of the thistle he eats". You almost never meet *real* fakirs. Imagine me, at diplomatic receptions in our Capital, dressed in evening dress, talking Western languages. Can I talk about the *real* things of life when the only Western people of spirituality are, to us, themselves odd and greedy people? No, of course not. So I say nothing. But in the assembly of such a man as our host here, *here* I can be of some use. And he can be of use to me, for it is from him that I gain my *baraka,* the power of the Teachers and the great ones of the present, the past and the future.'

He shook my hand, got up and left.

A servant came up, and announced that the Sufi Chief whom we had been discussing had arrived. A moment later he was brought in, following another Nubian. He was tall, thin, with a prominent nose and thick black hair. He looked like a Spanish aristocrat is supposed to look. He was wearing a sober European suit of very good cut, and on his head was a small red skullcap. Smiling he shook hands with all present, some of whom evidently knew him well. There was undoubtedly something very striking about him – what people call 'personality' when they cannot explain it. He sat down on the edge of a sofa, and was silent.

'Hadrat,' said our host, 'please take some coffee, honour us.' He spoke in English. The Sufi nodded, and answered in perfect English, 'Thanks very much, I will.'

Perhaps in order to forestall a rush of questions, Khalid said to the teacher, 'We have been talking about the so-called miracles and their relationship with ordinary life. Could you comment upon this subject?' Himself a patrician born and bred, he obviously held the Sufi in great esteem.

'Miracles,' the other immediately said, 'miracles are happening every day. Today we can do scientific things which would have been considered inexplicable in the recent past. This is a truism, of course. But the same is true of the human brain, let us call it that. The difference is that to do what you call miracles, *muajizat* in Arabic, we have to use ourselves as the machine. In this field, the field of human relations, we cannot use dead machines. People don't like to use themselves, because they have already been trained to enjoy external impacts or internal satisfactions. The possibility of using the human organism for a constructive purpose does not appeal to them.'

'You mean that they do not know how they can develop themselves? And if you were to tell them, they would not do it.'

There was a silence.

'Why would they not do it?' demanded the middle-aged man.

'Because they have to give you a fair hearing. This hearing is listening to words, seeing things, feeling things, doing things. The people have been trained to believe that anything that can be *done* is either inborn – like a talent – or can be learned by the *stringing together of a number of words*. This is one of the grossest impositions which have ever been perpetrated. The other, perpetrated by the "psychic" school, is that the goal can be attained merely by *thinking* certain things, or doing things which are variously described as "meditation", "concentration", "contemplation" or what-have-you.'

'Is this connected with human experience?' the painter wanted to know, 'because if it is, surely human experiences can be passed from one person to another : I try to do this with my art.'

'My dear friend. Your art may be perfect in itself. We are not discussing that. I will return to it if you like. But almost all artists are merely the forerunners of the mass-communications media. They may transmit, convey experience in one form, but this is not active but vicarious experience. To us, you see, art is not the ability to stimulate certain emotions. It is the ability to share feelings and also living, living. I show you a photograph of a cartoon and you smile. I show you a television programme and you laugh or cry. Is that living life, is that contributing to life? You may feel, of couse, that this has a function : it makes people happy or relaxed. It also dwarfs their intellect, robs them of volition.'

CHAPTER TEN

The Murshid Speaks

'Come to see me at any time' the Sufi chief had said, and I took him up on it. The next morning he and Khalid were sitting together talking about the previous night's visits to distribute *baraka* here and there; for all the world like Haroun el Raschid and his Vizier in old Baghdad.

I had just been reading the newspapers from London, full of reports and talk about juvenile delinquency. This might be a good subject to tackle. 'What do you think about the reform of criminals and the problem of juvenile delinquency?' I asked as soon as we were settled. The Sufi and Khalid exchanged glances.

'Are you sure,' said Khalid, 'that you have not been listening to gossip, or are you psychic?'

It appeared that, several months before, in great secrecy, the force of *baraka* had been used to transform (that is the only word) refractory prisoners in a gaol. Out of those discharged, none had come back yet. And the troublesome ones had been as calm as lambs ever since. Khalid stressed that this was a very unofficial experiment, because the authorities would not approve. Exactly why not was unclear. Juvenile delinquency was another cause that the Murshid had very much at heart. He had treated, it seemed, a large number of the children of well-to-do families and these had been found to be more in need of treatment than those from poorer families. There were cases of theft, robbery with violence, persistent car-stealing, forgery and 'various forms of viciousness'. No failures had been reported.

'But he will not take any money,' said the practical Khalid, ruefully; 'all he will do is designate a charity. I have known him tell someone to send money to this or that poor person. But I keep asking him to set up a centre where this work can be done.'

'All in good time' said the Sufi, 'but it is not yet. When the time comes, it will be done.'

'We have people writing from the United States, from Switzerland. Where can you attend your cases if you have no centre? We cannot simply say "Our master is a wanderer; he has no headquarters. If he happens to be there when you need him, he will serve you." '

'Each case is decided on its merits' said the Shah; 'there is no theoretical case, you know. If I have to go to Yokohama' – the name of a town he often used to denote distance – 'I would do so if I felt that I had to do so.'

'And what about rejuvenation?' demanded Khalid. 'Do you know' he said to me, 'how many people have their ageing processes slowed down, *actually* live longer, much longer, through the relaxation and special exercises which the Sufis use? These things are in everyday use. Think of the value of this factor alone in the service of humanity.'

'If you were under my discipline,' said the Sufi with a wink at me, 'I would forbid you to behave in such a disrespectful manner. There is almost nowhere that these practices would not be considered rank charlatanry. There is no unprejudiced hearing possible, because we work, we do not experiment. What sort of an answer is that for a scientific man? Every doctor in the world would be after our blood if we used the methods outside our own preserve. That is to say, if they were to work outside our own field. *Baraka* is one thing; it is a force, almost a physical one. Co-operation, working together in Sufic techniques, is needed in longevity. Unless and until it forms itself, naturally, this form of therapy cannot be popularised.

'But it may die out' wailed Khalid.

'Nothing worthwhile dies out, nor *can* it die out. There always have been, and always will be, Sufis. They carry the torch. If you knew what you were talking about, you would know that.'

I asked Khalid why he did not become a disciple. 'I have tried. He won't have me.'

'Of course I won't have you. Some people think that all they have to do is to sign on a dotted line. They have to be suitable. You are a dear friend, but you are not ready yet.'

It surely must be only in Sufism, I thought as I scribbled a shorthand note, that a mystical teacher can have a friendship on so cordial a basis with someone who is not of his community.

'Why are you always writing down?' Khalid was depressed.

'You want to learn. Learning comes through action as well as listening and seeing. How much of this can you absorb or communicate through words?'

'He cannot communicate it through words.' The teacher looked straight at me as he spoke. 'He is trying. He wants to be a writer. When he gives this up, he will be a Sufi. I think he will make a good Sufi. At the moment he is preparing himself. But he will be able to extend no *baraka,* arrive at no true end, until he forgets the words, just as you forget the letters when you are reading a word.'

'Will you stop me writing?' I asked him.

'No, but your book or your writing is not going to be what you think it is. Remember that the experience cannot be conveyed. I imagine that you are trying to see whether you can find a new dimension in literature: trying to convey the Sufi message. It has never been done, you know. At the best you will have a slightly disconnected series of images.'

'Will this be of no use to others?'

'Yes, it will be of use, but the only permanent usefulness is that which you yourself know to be a usefulness. The mere fact that you had to ask me the question shows that you do not know. Before you can do a thing you must *know;* and know in a very special sense.'

I knew, in a way, what he meant. The problem of conveying this to an outside audience was sometimes almost more than I could bear. But I felt very strongly, I would not say I knew, that I should try. My first master at Kunji Zagh had said: 'Sincerity will compensate for a great deal of inadequacy – use, live it.'

'A book,' Shah said, after a silence, 'may be written for one reason and understood in another sense. You find this problem in scholasticism and in book reviews. A reviewer may see a book in a different way from another reviewer. I do not mean that one reviewer will like a book, another hate it. I mean that the actual experience of the book will differ from one person to another. And this may merely be a work of entertainment. In the case of a book which is written to convey certain meanings, the influence upon the reader may be other than he actually thinks.'

'He may be influenced by a book without knowing it?'

'He may be influenced, as you put it, in a way other than he thinks.'

'Does all the book influence him in the same way?'

'It depends upon the book. You may not be able to conceive it, but a book may be written with the intention of conveying one, just one, objective fact. The rest of the book may be worthless, though it may be entertaining and apparently good or convincing.'

'Does this apply to the various scriptures?'

'Yes, it applies to some. But the alterations and editing which has gone into most of the world's scriptures, the tailoring to accord with dogma, has virtually eliminated the understanding of the message. The sense may be restored by an intuitive person; but then the book might not even be recognizable as the same book.'

'Is this what the Sufis mean by their very far-reaching statement: "We have taken the kernel of the Koran and rejected the husk?"'

'Partially, in that the Koran contains materials for Sufi "work". Ritual, as you know, is generally a survival of the mind-action combination. Hence, when the Koran is read it is read in one of certain tones of voice, and certain passages are read at certain times. This part of the activity is in addition to the formal as well as the symbolic meaning of the text.'

'Do you find a similar hidden meaning in the Christian scriptures?'

'Certainly, at times.'

Would he, I asked him, combine certain physical movements and certain music; certain ideas, with the contemplation of pictures; would this be a part of self-work, the kind of human activity that was a part of the inner Sufism?

'This is a part of Sufism.'

'So any or all of the impacts which affect the lives of all of us can be considered as possibly shaping us towards the development which the Sufis call the Complete Man?'

'This is an integral part of Sufi teaching. It is only the fact that external impacts as well as internal thinking have already to some extent shaped man and woman that they are in any way accessible to the Sufi teaching. The work has already started, long before the Sufi contact is made.'

'On that basis you would say that the Sufi impact started before the complicated exercises which are used by the Sufis?'

'Sufism always existed, for all practical purposes. The exercises are designed to bring the practitioner back to a truly Sufic condition, following and correcting the chance impacts which have partially influenced him away from the Sufi way of thought and action.'

'So they are a corrective as much as a system of development?'

'You cannot separate the one from the other. You cannot build a castle on mud-flats; but with the human being you can give him support while you are helping him to overcome the wrong kind of development.'

I asked him what relationship the wonders and miracles ascribed to the Sufis had to the philosophy and the conviction that the Sufi was developing in accordance with an evolutionary need.

'You cannot separate the wonders from the development. The so-called "psychic powers" are a by-product of Sufi work. They are never actually sought by the Sufi; they happen. But they, like everything else in the Sufi's life, are of some importance. They develop as a result of an evolutionary need. The Sufi needs them in order to carry out his mission. He cannot use them "to order" as it were, because he is operating on a higher plane. It may be permissible for a wedding-cake to be cut with a sword intended for killing an enemy – perhaps, but it is certainly wrong for a thing to be put to a use which is not in harmony with its real use.'

'Is the example of the sword not a wrong use, then?'

'I saw it done, once; that is why I mention it. I realised then that this particular sword was not significant, and could be used in this way. Its real use will depend upon someone knowing through an instinctive knowledge what its real use is. This is why we have to be careful of the theoretical instances.'

'Tell me more about the transmission of meanings' I asked 'because this is something which is difficult to grasp if we try to think it out.'

'It is difficult to grasp because you automatically test every thought against what you have already been taught, by a variety of equally insensitive theorists. If you do not allow the picture to build up gradually, you will find that you will either accept everything credulously (which is terrible and can produce a mealy-mouthed do-gooder) or you will take everything in little bits, split up by your mind and interpreted by your own apparatus. This interpretation, when you try to unify it again, will produce a false view of the whole question. However, I will just mention one or two aspects of this:

'A book, as we have said, may convey meanings other than what appears on the surface. A conversation may take place to convey an experience other than that of its apparent content. A man may tell you a story in which certain emotions are mixed. Do you remember the story or are you influenced by the emotions; or do you simply learn facts, or what? To the Sufis, a conversation will tend to be complete: to reach you from different directions and on several levels. Parables are a simple form of this kind of teaching.

'A seemingly casual happening will have one meaning for one person, another for another. No happening is accidental in the crude sense in which we understand the word "accident". Hence a Sufi happening, as you might call it, is intended, if that is the right word, to affect everyone concerned, each in his own way.'

'Yes, I can see that' I told him, 'someone said: "Two men looked out from prison bars, one saw mud, the other stars." '

'That is the kind of thing, and you often find it in poetry. It is not so easy to spot it in events, however. People puzzle over events, and philosophers try to explain happenings in a way which will accord with their theories. We, you see, have no theories in that sense. This is because we are attuned to happenings, and get the message from them.'

'Well, if you will clarify a little. Suppose we take the couplet about the stars and prison bars' I said, as I wanted to know whether I understood this properly, 'and consider this as a happening. How does it affect us as Sufis, in addition to the way in which the ordinary person understands it?'

'We will not bother for the moment how the ordinary person understands it, though we may return to it later. It affects the Sufi in direct relationship to the Sufi's position on the Sufi Way. We believe that it really affects everyone in this sense, because as it is an experience it must vary in impact according to the state of the individual.'

'Is it of value to the ordinary person, who has no Sufi awareness?'

'Very little. You see, such sentiments when once they have been expressed, become what we call "worn out". They become truisms; things repeated mechanically. They are tags, and they have tags attached to them. People carry on whole conversations in proverbs. But they are not *living* the proverbs. Proverbs and truisms are for this reason dangerous, because they produce blindness or non-thought. When you get a principle on which everyone is agreed, you get the beginning of complacency and deterioration. Nobody will oppose the principle of "peace for all the world". Believing that they believe in this, they have to do nothing about it. Oh, yes, I know that they talk about it, keep the matter in the headlines. But they do not apply the essential character of peace to themselves as individuals. They now regard "peace" as something which applies to groups of people, not to the individual. This is why there can be no real peace, only the absence of actual fighting. But peace is more than that.'

'How do you view members of political parties, then, who campaign for certain principles?'

'Just the same way as I view any other human being. They are no different because they are members of political movements. This is what people do not understand, and it does not take a Sufi to tell them : people are people. People think that they can campaign for or against something in their capacity as "ordinary folk". It is just because they are such "ordinary folk" that they fall into the hands of politicians who divert everything to different ends. If the "ordinary folk" would make themselves worthwhile, then they would be able to guide affairs, not just form the cannon-fodder. But this is not easy. It is easier to work on the primitive level, to arrange a mass rally and demonstrate than to improve oneself.'

'The question of the quality of the individual?'

'Yes. You see, if I take a bag of rotten apples and say that these apples must have justice, that is one thing. If I say that they are entitled, because they are apples, merely because they were created as apples, to be made into a delicious apple sauce, I am out of harmony with reality.'

'But is this not a doctrine of the élite?'

'It is, with the difference that we are *all* the élite, if we only knew it. The illiterate, one-eyed weakling is worth just as much as the towering, well-developed ideal man of externals. They are both entitled to what they deserve. And what they deserve is a matter of their inner regeneration. You see, people demand so much. They do not contribute enough. They think of what they want, not what they must give. They do not know that in giving there is self-development and progress.'

'Is this not a religious doctrine?'

It is a religious doctrine, but in religion it is only passed on in partial form.'

'Just before I left England,' I said, 'there was a burst of the perennial discussion as to how to attract better school-teachers into the profession. How would you answer that? Most people seemed to say that they should be better paid, on the argument that a man should not have to suffer because he had a vocation for teaching, and that people with a general vocation for service would be attracted to teaching because better pay meant that they would be able to discharge their familiy responsibilities. Surely this is a good basis for progress?'

'Yes, excellent, if you are attacking the thing externally. You do not notice that in teaching, as with everything else, the essential point is the regeneration of the teacher. You want better teachers. You must provide conditions which will produce better people, some of whom will become teachers. It is not a question of "people with a general vocation for service"; it is a matter of producing a consciousness of vocation. You have to produce better people. Remember, the man or woman who has the best developed essence will undoubtedly prevail. This is called "personality" and so on. It is the outer manifestation of the inner perfection.

'In the West you generally get people partially developed. They will of course prevail over the less-developed ones. But since they have no idea of being in harmony with evolution, this development will sometimes become harnessed to negative ideals. These are ideals which are in the end undesirable.'

This conversation had taken up almost the whole morning, and after lunch I asked some questions on Sufi organisation, something of a delicate point, because Sufis are organised in a manner inexplicable to the outsider.

'Our organisation is like our system,' the master told me, 'and that is to say it exists but is not used, as you would say, until it is needed. It does not resemble a formal organisation because it is not based upon mechanical principles.'

'But suppose one Sufi has to take over from another, does he operate entirely upon intuition? I have been told that Sufi masters have sent their disciples to distant lands to take the place of a master who has died, for instance. Does this mean that there is a telepathic communication between all Sufis?'

'You are still trying to force us into someone else's pattern,' he was amused and showed it. 'We do not work like that. If there is what you might call a vacuum somewhere, a Sufi will have to fill it. The manner of its filling may take many forms. I was once sent to fill a gap such as you describe; but there is a great deal of intuition involved, so it will take what seems to be different forms according to the circumstances.'

'When you enter a group of Sufis, do you know instinctively how far they have progressed, and what their potentialities are?'

'In many cases, yes. But it is not always necessary, because the Sufic progress is taking place in any case, through the inner harmony of the group. Do not think that the Sufi is a man with a permanently open line of communication with transcendental knowledge. This is not how the thing works, otherwise we would all be trying to become illuminated sages with all knowledge. This would make us like the people of the Far East, who want to become gods or something.'

'But you use formulas and signs and identification-signals.'

'Yes, we do, and how they are used tells us something about each other. Here is an example. You know a password. You come to a meeting, and tell it to me. You may think that this password tells me your grade or importance. In actual fact it tells me a great deal of things. When you say it, how you say it, and so on, creates the impression in my mind that I need in order to assess you.'

'Could this be the original derivation of passwords and secret signs?'

'I am sure that it is.'

'What about special circumstances, when a Sufi wants to convey a meaning to another one who belongs to another Order, or who has to carry on his work? Is that covered by the intuitive use of signals which were designed for other purposes?'

'Nothing is "designed for other purposes". You can have a

phrase with objective, consistent meaning, which will come into operation when the time is ready.'

'How does this work?'

'It cannot be explained, but an instance can be given. My teacher gave me a watchword, and I don't mind telling you what it is – a Sufi secret is not in mere words. This was the phrase *Eea Shahim Sahist*. This phrase means. "O Shah, it is prepared". This is a recognition-signal, inasmuch as a group which is waiting for me in a place will say it to me, more as a greeting than anything else. It is a phrase used in handing over a command, as it were.

'It has a great many significances, most of which operate only on the intuitive plane. But, if we look at it as far as we can through superficial eyes, we will learn something at least. In the first place it is a Persian phrase, which is in standard use with Sufis : Persian of the classical sort is their basic language. But it has been so arranged as to be intelligible to an Arab or a Turk, especially a Turk. That is to say, it contains words common to those languages, and no word which is not common to the three languages. It would also be understood by a person who knows Urdu. This, in a sense, defines a part of one's territory. I do not operate in China you see, or Japan, and so on.

'The wording is such that it connotes an act of handing over. This means that to a group which has this word, I am, in an *outer* sense, appointed to direct them. This direction might have taken place without the word, but the ratification of the taking-over is in this word. I, in turn, have a phrase which I leave with my group before I complete my mission, when the time comes to settle in one place. Until then the phrase may be used by me for a different purpose, or it may be concealed. This is governed by my intuition. If I meet a Sufi and use the phrase *Eea Shahim,* he will reply, if he is not of my "flock" a certain word which is generally known to us. If he is one of the group in which I have a duty, he will perhaps complete the phrase. So the sentence has both an initiatory and superficial use.'

'Suppose you have a group to visit, and they have lost the "word" – what happens then?'

'This is theory again. For practical purposes the word is not lost. If a great period of time intervenes between one teacher and the next, the group will have lost its advantages of development.

It will be like a photographic plate which has been developed but not fixed. This means that in the absence of the teacher the teachings, the evolution, is fading. Hence, if the word fades too, it would be natural. The word would not be needed any more, because the next teacher would have to start from scratch in any case.'

'But if, as I have been told, your province lies in the West, how do Persian words apply? Or do you operate in groups of people of Eastern extraction?'

'My dear fellow, I have no idea. You keep on asking things that may or may not be happening. We deal in things as they happen. I know that we say "Do not be a man of the past, be a man of the present and of the future", but it has to be a future that is real, not just imagined.'

'So there may be quite a number of esoteric groups which have lost the word, or who are carrying on rituals whose meaning is an inner one, and which they have forgotten. Rituals for which they have produced a meaning, but which is not the original meaning?'

'The world is littered with them, and littered is the word.'

'Do you recognise them?'

'From time to time we come across them. Often you can do nothing, because they have been transformed. They are merely self-perpetuating organisations. People take them for the real thing. Rumi said, if you remember: "It is only because there is such a thing as real gold that people are taken in by the counterfeit".'

I reverted to the question of the 'secret word' which had so many meanings. 'Could I ask something about the identification phrase?'

'Ask anything.'

'How are the phrases worked out?'

'Sometimes by the numerical value of the letters. Sometimes otherwise. Take my phrase. Without going into the mathematical side, let us suppose that I want to send a message to someone by a non-Sufi, and I want to authenticate its origin. I may have to send it to someone with whom I have no strong Sufi connection, but who will understand my "phrase". I write it down letter by letter or syllable by syllable, on seperate pieces of paper. Rearranging the sounds, I get – if I use the Arabic letters – the phrase *Hashim hiss eea sihat*. This is almost meaningless, so he rearranges them, and gets my phrase. Of course, if I were using Latin letters, I would rearrange in a slightly different way, because in the Perso-Arabic alphabet as you know, the letter H is sometimes pronounced as A, and so on.'

'So it is a kind of password – system?'

'Yes, but much more than that. This is something which cannot be explained in all its aspects, as I have already said.'

'It sounds to me something like the theory of the "magic word" which so many occultists use.'

'It is a bit like that, but it is not "magic." Magic is not what it seems, and that is what keeps the wrong sort of people busy with it, and away from anything else. Formerly this kind of person sought power through magic. Nowadays he is more likely to see it through what are called in English "causes". There is nothing like a "cause" to obscure the need for self-improvement and to try to attain something without working in the right manner.'

CHAPTER ELEVEN

Nasnas and Wiswas

What did the Shah think about other schools of mysticism? There were in Britain and in perhaps most other countries, schools and teachers, organisations arranged around some central idea, or following the teachings of some master, alive or dead. If we were to assume that some were false, their followers were deluded. If we were to believe that some were true, others partially true, yet others less true in their ideas, where did the Sufi way fit in with it all?

I felt this problem very keenly, though I had not been in intimate contact with any group. I had my own ideas by now as to what sort of pattern might in fact underlie the various expressions of mysticism, the numerous followings. But I wanted urgently to have an answer from the Sufi source.

He seemed to welcome my query. 'The answer,' he said, 'is so very much simpler than you think, and this is merely because you are thinking in a number of circles. Each circle communicates, and thoughts chase one another around, from circle to circle. I can give you your answer; but I cannot guarantee that you will understand it.'

Any system which was what he called "tight", tightly organised on the basis of certain principles and which developed only within them, he said, was wrong. There was no such thing as bringing mysticism into the field of the 'applied sciences' as one would learn, say, mechanics or farming. It had too many dimensions. But there were schools which taught by means of specific principles, and which made their followers adhere to these. In false or deluded schools ('remnant cults' was the name he liked giving the latter) the system had become the 'prison of the people'. A child, he reminded me, might have to be placed in a small playpen, to protect it and also to develop it. The pen had certain advantages, certain faculties. For instance, some playpens had built into their sides such things as an abacus, for playing or counting beads. The playpen might be an essential part of the equipment of the home, of the facilities for the child, of the stage of development. Now, when the child became bigger . . . the playpen became a prison.

How did one know when one was in a playpen and when not?

'We are all in playpens, most of the time,' he explained. 'What we must look at is the objective. The objective of the pen was to preserve and develop the child. The function of the parent was to rear the child so that it could eventually be liberated, and become a fully-grown and free adult. This is the objective of the teacher. When the child grows up, it is independent of the adult. This is the objective of growing up.

It was not necessary to worry as to whether a mystical society was totally false, partially false, or anything else, when it was considered from the point of view of liberation and completion. What mattered was : 'Does the teacher deliver the goods?' Look at your society and ask yourself the question : 'Does this school produce better people? Are they made independent of the school, so that they can go their way, in turn completed and developed?' If the answer is 'NO', then the system is failing. Why it is failing is not so important, because tinkering with it will not put it right. It can be righted only by a Master.

I was deeply impressed by these words, because they faced squarely the statement that the proof of the pudding is in the eating. They showed me how to assess a school, and warned not to be side-tracked by words.

'We must not fail to see' he continued, 'the fact that any system, any form of belief, however slight, can produce great results. The question is not, as so many people ask : "Is this school not to be considered true, because of such and such a result?" The question is, rather : "Are these results permanent? Do they lead to the *detachment,* not the *attachment* of the individual? Has inner regeneration taken place? Are the people who are being regenerated apparently improved, or the sort of people who give *me* a sensation of hope and the possibility of fulfillment?" '

These remarks were shot out at such speed that I had difficulty in taking them down in shorthand, at which I was fairly proficient.

Above all, he stressed, it will be necessary to note whether the development of the members of the group is taking place in accordance with balance. It is easy to train people, sometimes easier than it is to train animals. Trained people are people who have been given an impression, a 'conditioning' which makes them 'lean on one side'. The training always takes the form of concentration upon one thing. This is all very well: concentration upon oneself, upon a principle, and so on. But have the people been given detachment and also concentration in a balanced way upon the rest of humanity?

It was quite obvious that these tests, if applied to many, very many, of the followers of various mystical schools, would show that they were, at the best, often merely imitators, or people who thought that they were 'getting somewhere' but who showed by their not being 'rounded' that they were developing, if at all, eccentrically.

'When we talk about the Perfect Man, which is also translatable as the Complete Man, we are not just spouting nonsense, you know. Complete means complete; perfect means perfect. Any approach to either of these ideas does not allow for unbalance, for one-sided development.'

'Why did Sufis not oppose any other mystical school?'

There were several very good reasons. In the first place, the Sufi is fully engaged on Sufism. Secondly, other schools often provided some sort of introduction to the spirit of mysticism. At the very least they served in some places as a representative of mysticism. They might be wrong, they might get into bad odour; but some more sensitive people would see in them the echo of something: 'If there were no true gold, people would not accept counterfeit.'

So there was no point in saying that this school was better than that, for instance. Many followers of other schools were obsessed. You cannot meet an obsessed person head-on to any useful purpose.

There was no harm in looking at some of the other cults, he said, no harm at all. If one were attracted by them, so much the better, in a way, because the conflict would bring out the 'reality'. In conflict the individual would realise whether he should join the one or the other. If he joined the non-Sufi school, all the better for all concerned.

'So you don't try to save souls?'

'We do not try to save souls.'

I reverted to the 'remnant cults' – he gave me various examples. One was the image of a fire-making religion on a remote island. One day an advanced man arrived at this island, perhaps a castaway. With him he had a box of matches. When the savages who lived there saw him using them to make fire, they concluded that he was some sort of a god. They set up a shrine to him. He, realising that his safety perhaps depended upon their fearing or respecting him, allowed them to do this. People came and worshipped at the shrine. When he died, the empty matchbox remained as the altar, and a religion was established. This is one way in which a 'matchbox cult' could grow up.

'We must always remember the difficulty that the ordinary man or woman has in interpreting the behaviour of the stranger, even if he is an illuminated man.'

Then there were the cults which used fixed rituals, mere pantomime, to represent beliefs. Their origin, as likely as not, had been flexible, in the Sufi sense. People had been given things to think, to do and to believe, until such time as they were sufficiently developed to do, think and experience other things. He would not name any specific cult, but a little reflection brought several to my mind as possible illustrations.

Then there were the cults which were built up on a knowledge of certain 'natural laws'. In ancient times priests were the only people allowed to know certain facts which are today common-places of scientific knowledge. Imagine, for instance, that there was a firemaking cult, and only the priesthood could make fire. They might be deceiving the people in reserving this function to themselves. On the other hand, they might genuinely believe that only they should make fire, because the taboo had never been broken since the first man made it, and thought himself to be specifically gifted in a supernatural way. He passed on his secret, perhaps in good faith.

There were healing cults, which performed cures by suggestion. The value of these was at last being recognised by science, and many strange experiments had been performed by American hypnotherapists. Some of them, in published papers, were at the moment only hinting at the possibilities; but clearly they were hinting. Cults could be created on less. But the mistake was to think that the use of this power, this healing faculty which was scientific enough, when one was 'blind' to its inner reality, was enough.

'You know how there are legends in all sorts of places, about power being dangerous as well as useful? How a person is given a power by a magician subject to terrible provisions? That is only an allegorical way of saying something else. If you hypnotise a person, as you can surely do, without being in contact with the real experience of hypnosis, you are adversely affecting the balance of the power. I cannot be more clear, I am afraid. But it is like a man using fire to heat his kettle, and then not noticing that it can also burn his carpet, or his hand.'

Did he mean that straightforward use of hypnosis was dangerous?

'Absolutely. Not in the way that people think it is, you see. If you merely hypnotise someone in order to cure something, and you do not also exert your conscious *baraka* upon that person, all sorts of things might happen. You have removed, say, the stammer that your patient was suffering from. But you get other symptoms instead. This much is understood by some hypnotists, so they get round that – and it is quite possible. What they do not know is that unless they attain a complete *baraka* relationship with their patient, they will influence his evolutionary powers adversely.'

'But how can this be learned? And how does the Sufi apply it when he is healing someone?'

'The Sufi has it anyway. He cannot hypnotise anyone without making a mystical contact, as it were. It is not learned, it is experienced.'

It was shortly after this that an amusing event showed something of the difference of hypnotism from what Sufis called hypnosis, but which they consider to be something else. I was writing some notes in the patio one afternoon, unheeding of the buzz of conversation of the usual throng of visitors. Then a middle-aged woman came and sat beside me, and spoke to me in French. I had not seen her before. She was asking whether the 'Maitre' was at home. I went up to the small room where the mystic carried out his afternoon meditation, and found him there. Before I had time to say anything, he said: 'Tell her her husband will be completely well tomorrow.' Almost automatically I went downstairs again, and repeated the message to the lady in French. She was alarmed: 'He is a magician? I never mentioned my husband. I wanted to ask him about myself, and to see whether he had any supernatural powers.'

Her husband had been spitting blood, and feared that he had tuberculosis, which was in the family already. She was very worried about him, and had heard of the healing powers available here from someone in a shop. Her husband was to have an X-ray photograph taken that afternoon, was having a siesta and she had crept away to see whether anything could be done.

'If you are a Catholic, Madame,' I could not resist saying to her, 'you must know something of the powers of the holy to cure all illnesses.'

The next day there was a note from the woman, a mixture of joy and fear, which I transcribed.

'Maitre – I cannot see you, though I would very much like to do so. My husband is well again, so soon, and there was nothing on the radiological film. I am so happy and I thank you, but I beg of you to consider the grace of Our Lady, before it is too late, I would not presume to say this unless I were grateful and wished to share my joy. We leave this evening, so adieu.'

'What did you use?' I asked; 'hypnosis, telepathy, healing, what?'

'I used the *amal*' he said in Persian. The word means 'work', and in the language in which the answer was given (although we generally talked in English) it has a special Sufi meaning of producing a result by a power of concentration, an inner concentration which is not defined by any special term.

I suppose that it is natural to be impressed by seeming wonders, and this is somethting that a person almost seems to crave for. In any case, I excitedly awaited any further objective evidence of some mechanism that might be working.

The same day Khalid came in and, just as he was starting to say something the Sufi interrupted: 'The child is dead, but the mother will survive and have more children; and all will be well.'

This statement, as I was soon to learn, referred to a woman who was about to have a child which was to be a difficult birth, the wife of a close friend of Khalid's. He had been about to describe the situation and ask for help.

I expressed a wish to be able to develop powers like these.

'It is easier to develop the powers of *wiswas* and *nasnas*' the mystic said. Without waiting to be asked what they were, he told me that there was a stage of confusion of mind which could be induced in other people, which sometimes came of itself. This was *wiswas,* and mentioned in Sufi books. Then there was the state called *nasnas.* This is caused through what is called 'fixation'. One person, if he can summon up enough nervous energy, can work on the nervous system of a sensitive person in such a way as to make this individual react. The reaction takes the form of shuddering and later illusions in which the person believes himself to be an animal, or behaves like one. He referred me to a passage in a book by the Sufi teacher Hujwiri on this.

He believed, interestingly enough, that the complaint which so many Malays suffer from – Latah – was connected with the belief in were-tigers and so on. Latah is a form of nervous compulsive imitation which can be set off by a surprise, or by fear. Many Europeans had been trained to develop it, sometimes as a party joke, especially in Malay and Borneo. Javanese magicians often used this predeliction, as they did the ritual of the 'calling down the monkey-spirit' into people, to reinforce their curative claims. It is undesirable to produce either Latah or *nasnas* in anyone, though he did know healers who did it. The inner part of the mind, while unable to prevent itself from being put into a state of *nasnas,* rebelled against the operator, and would as a result in turn cause debility in him. Some women drove their husbands out of their minds by this technique, which had been demonstrated by a Hindu to our teacher. The Hindu had spent much time in Ceylon and Indonesia.

'It is a shocking sight,' he told me, 'and anyone who was, shall we say, emotionally uncommitted, might follow such a *guru* for years because of the shock which he had received.'

I did not ask to be initiated into *nasnas,* or latah either.

A few days later the secretary of a society which interested itself in various forms of what might be called occultism, called to pay his respects. His members, he said, would be more than gratified if they could be received and given a lecture dealing with problems which exercised the minds of all deep thinkers. He was referring, he said, to such questions as survival after death, reincarnation, paranormal powers, spiritualism in general, the true and the false in the occult. He was a widely-read man gentle in demeanour, and had lived many years in America. His society was in touch with many organisations in the West, including the United States and Germany. They had sent representatives to 'gatherings of mystics', and practised a form of spiritual healing for which they claimed good results. They believed in the essential unity of all religion. Beyond the latter requirement, any opinions could be held by members.

Our Sufi closed his eyes for a moment, then opened them and looked the seeker of wisdom straight in the eyes. 'Are you prepared to hear what I say, right to the end?'

'Oh, yes, indeed; more than prepared. That is what we want. The Sufis who go about Syria will not talk to us, or else they give inexplicable answers.'

So the meeting was fixed for a week later, to be held in the courtyard of the mansion.

When the day arrived, the lecturer went out, as he often did, and Khalid and I wondered whether he had forgotten the time. People started to arrive half an hour before the time of the meeting. Eventually there were about sixty, sitting on chairs and sofas, cushions and ledges, conversing in low tones. They seemed a cosmopolitan lot, of all ages, both sexes, all in Western clothes, women preponderant.

Precisely at the moment when the lecture was scheduled to begin, the lecturer walked into the courtyard. He looked at the society's secretary, nodded, said 'What language?'

'Everyone can manage in English,' said the official.

Standing in the middle of his audience, the teacher immediately started to speak:

'Welcome. For as far back as there is any recorded history, people have been interested in two things: whether they would survive death, and seemingly occult phenomena. Students of humanity in every branch of science and scholastic discipline have tried to account for this interest. The method which most people seem to adopt in their search for the answers to the questions implicit in the two forms of interest to which I have referred has usually been the same. This method is to seek out things which seem to indicate the supernatural. Then the phenomena are studied and attempts are made to create or duplicate these phenomena. Alternatively, people who seem to control or to be controlled by their phenomena, to whatever degree, are sought and followed. One moment's thought, which few people will spare in their eagerness to find something out, would show the weakness of this method of approaching the supernatural phenomenon. I therefore invite you to ask yourselves, individually and collectively, what method you have established that you are competent to judge either theories or so-called proofs.

'This has never been established. The method which you are using is to try to understand something by means of something which is not objective: your ordinary, or even abnormal, mind.

'The Sufis in general will not discuss these matters with people who are not Sufis. The reason is that if they did, the non-Sufis would consider that they were mad; and the Sufis would be able to make no progress. Few people in their right minds would attempt to discuss, or evaluate, nuclear physics without preparation for the task. Yet almost every human being feels that he can have a reasonable opinion about the supernatural. He asks for information, it is true, for phenomena, for tales and demonstrations. But he does not ask for basic training to enable him to understand. This is like the child who goes to a school for the first time and expects to be taught a foreign language at an advanced level, without having any basic knowledge about that language, and what makes it up.

'The child is, not unnaturally, impatient. This is a characteristic of children. He sees people talking in a foreign language, and wants to know one, too. He sees the wonder, but not the mechanism. He asks questions which have no answer which he would understand, like: "Who is the Moon?" or "Why are two and two not three?" The child, however, can be told by the teacher or parent that "It is so because it is so"; or "This does not matter at the moment – eat up your food". The "raw" seeker after supernatural truth *can,* of course, be told these things by a teacher. But, unlike the ordinary infant, he will drift away from the stern "parent" who talks like this. You can imagine the plight of the tiny infant who, instead of allowing the parent to discount his questionings, slips away and tries to live on his own: or seeks, every few days, another parent who will teach him the things he wants to know: not the things which he should be taught.'

He stopped speaking, abruptly. Although his words had been hard, his expression was benign and open. I felt a surge of sympathy, of friendship, for a man who did not deal in mystification, who was prepared to say precisely what he meant : who was not trying to attract followers or make a personal impression based on a claim to secret knowledge.

'Good night,' he said, and withdrew to his room. The lecture was over.

I looked round at the congregation. Some looked stunned; others chastened. One or two were talking together animatedly. 'Oh dear,' said a dear old lady sitting near me to her companion, 'I had so *many* questions to ask, all prepared.' She waved a dozen sheets of paper.

I said to Khalid : 'What did you think of it?'

He grinned. 'What makes you think that I am qualified to have an opinion.'

CHAPTER TWELVE

The Richest Man Alive

Through my Sufi friends I got an invitation to meet the Emir of Kuwait, Sheikh Abdallah el-Salem el-Sabah, whose tiny Persian Gulf kingdom lay above one of the largest oil deposits in the world. I had heard how Sheikh Abdallah was a sort of modern Haroun el-Raschid, how he had turned his country into a sort of paradise on earth, and how he helped people, all over the world, through a network of agents who literally had nothing else to do than ferret out really needy cases. Partly through the introduction which was offered me, partly through curiosity, partly in order to know his opinion of the Sufis, I jumped at the opportunity of visiting Kuwait.

As soon as I entered the departure lounge at Beirut International Airport an Iraqi and a Persian, who were to be among my travelling companions, started a conversation. Both were bitterly against Sheikh Abdallah. 'It is said,' claimed the Iraqi darkly, 'that he has helped even Jews, with this money of his. You know, of course, that Kuwait rightly belongs to Iraq, not to these illiterate beduins.'

'Oh, no, my friend,' chimed in the Persian, 'Kuwait is Persian, and it will be formally so before very long. Look at the number of Persians who are flooding in. They will overcome the Arab.'

Here, in a nutshell, was the basis of so much anti-Kuwait talk which is heard all over the Middle East. It is said that you have only to lend a man money to make an enemy of him. If this is so, then Kuwait must have plenty of enemies, because she had in the first few years of the nineteen sixties lent a colossal amount of money to Arab states.

I was whisked from Kuwait Airport, through neat rows of air-conditioned houses where desert had formerly been, to the unpretentious house where the Ruler lived. A tall, bulky figure, he came out himself to meet me, and took me to inspect the three rooms furnished in Arab style which had been put at my disposal.

I noted that the Sheikh was dressed in the robes of an ordinary beduin, and did not affect the gold head-dress which was his by right. In the street, apart from his commanding figure, he could have been mistaken for any ordinary son of the desert.

'Please join us for dinner' said the Sheikh, and left me with an interpreter and a refrigerator full of iced non-alcoholic drinks.

Dinner was straightforward Arab food, roast lamb and rice mainly, with various sauces and spiced meat-balls. The Ruler and about twenty of his friends sat around an oblong white cloth spread on the floor of a simply-furnished room. In conformity with Arab custom, not a word was spoken while we ate.

Afterwards, when our hands had been washed and the coffee cups were circulating, the Sheikh turned, almost abruptly, to me.

'I am an Arab, and we welcome you,' he said. 'But remember that we have been independent only since 1961. For many years before that we were accustomed to dealing with British people. We like them very much. We know they come to the point as soon as they can. I would like to do so with you, if this is what you want. If you want to know my income, it is over two hundred million sterling a year. If you want to know what I do with it, I have made this country, with God's help, the one with the best welfare state in the whole world. If you have a favour to ask, consider that I regard it as a favour to help you.'

I felt almost ashamed at his directness. Had I been trying to ask for money, I stuttered in Persian, this approach would have completely thrown me off balance.

The Sheikh laughed, and answered me in the same language.

'So you like Persian? Or your Arabic is weak? Never mind. But be assured that if you had come for money and had really needed it, we would already have known and would not have embarrassed you by talking in the way I have just spoken.'

I asked his highness how he felt about the Sufis assuming that he was not one of them.

'Most real Sufis,' he said, 'are seldom ever seen. This is because they are busy, they are at work. The others are busy trying to be Sufis, and it is those who are seen and who make a lot of noise.'

'Can you tell me something about them, and how they affect affairs?'

'I could tell you a great deal. The only difficulty is that you would not believe one-tenth of it. Here are some of the things which you may be able to believe, even though they go against your Western thoughts considerably.

'Among them, the junior is often more important than the senior, because rank by age or length of studies goes only in "blind" study, or in things of the world : like, for instance, the rulership of tribes.

'We must also distinguish between titular chiefs and real rulers. In a nation there is always a titular chief. Nowadays the ruler may be a figure-head, propped up by parliament. In ancient days it was the same, when someone powerful stood behind the nominal king and really ruled.

'In the case of the Sufis, there is a rulership, which jointly commands the whole organisation. The organisation is called the *Mu'assissa* (the Foundation). From time to time a "public chief" is selected by the *Mu'assissa*. Your friend al-Sayed Idries, al-Shah, is one such.'

I had never heard of this Foundation before, and asked the Ruler to tell me more about it. It was, he said, believed to have been founded several thousand years ago. Other versions were that it had always existed. Some said that it would always exist. Its objective was to look after the interests of all the people of the world.

'Even in the non-Moslem countries?'

'Of course. "All the people" means "all the people in the world." You must not be misled by the fact that people are collected together in nations and churches and organisations of one kind and another. The *Mu'assissa* operates through all of them, though the higher administration does not know it.'

'I suppose that your highness gives them money, for their work?'

'Only if they ask me. They have not asked me for very much. I wish that they would, but I have been entrusted with the task of making life as good as possible for my own people.'

'But you have a great surplus of capital?'

'Of course we have. We have something like six hundred million dollars invested in London at the moment. Many say that the City would collapse if we withdrew it, and it is for this reason that so many people attack us. They say we could manipulate British policy if we wanted to do so, by means of that weapon.'

'But you would not do so?'

'I am a Moslem, not a moneylender.'

'About the Sufis. How do they transmit instructions in their Foundation?'

'Every Sufi who is a senior member of the *Mu'assissa* is in spiritual touch with each other one. They work by understanding about what is needed, not by orders.

'So this *is* a spiritual movement?'

'Yes, it is.'

I asked the Ruler whether there was much Sufi activity in the West. He did not seem anxious to reply, but eventually he said: 'There is sufficient. It is everywhere.'

Obviously he approved of the Sufis. Was he to be considered as one of the important members of the *Mu'assissa*? 'No, just a well-wisher.'

If the Sufis asked him to do something, would he do it, no matter what it was?

'Whatever has to be done, will be done. Whatever cannot be done, or should not be done, will not be asked. It might just *appear* that things are asked, or that things should not or could not be done.'

Could the Sheikh tell me the names of any important member of the *Mu'assissa,* in the East or in the West?

'No, that, brother, I cannot. The present chief is the only one who is active. We need only one active one at a time. Until he becomes "inactive", the others remain "inert". You may not be able to follow me, but that is the best rendering I can give you.'

Would the Sheikh tell me anything about his activities in secret charity, because this was a concept so very unfamiliar to us in the West. We, after all, feel that there is no harm in charity being known, even if only because this helps others to be charitable. In fact, unless I was much mistaken, in most Western countries giving away money without keeping records would be considered illegal. A charity was, certainly in Britain, an institution which collected money and then gave it away under the supervision of the authorities.

'You surprise me' said the Sheikh; and then proceeded to surprise me even more.

'I have many times been told about one of your patron saints, St Nicholas. You celebrate his day at the same time as you celebrate the birth of the blessed Jesus. This Saint Nicholas was the man whom Christians remember best simply because he used to give secret charity. In doing so, he prevented certain recipients from becoming dissolute.'

I did not know much about St Nicholas, but pressed the Sheikh for further information.

'You see, if you give charity and know that the person to whom you give knows, you risk his feeling obligated to you. It is bad enough, surely, to be in the position of giving at all, and realising that you may merely be giving because it makes you feel happy. You are being rewarded for your action, instead of helping others without any reward. *I* call public giving, or even giving which is recorded anywhere, as a shameful and degenerate thing. Giving makes a man to be called "good". No man is "good" in that sense. If you want to be good, first find out whether you can be good without emotion. Then find out if you can be good without others knowing that you are good. If people think you are good, they are judging, you are making them judge you. This in itself is wrong.'

I was deeply affected by the Sheikh's interpretation. I caught the aircraft for Cairo, where I was to meet his Agent, in a very much humbler frame of mind.

CHAPTER THIRTEEN

Suleiman Bey

Sheikh Sabah had an Ambassador in Egypt, but the man whom he called his 'Agent' was Suleiman Bey, who met me at the airport in a chauffeur-driven car with cold soft drinks in its special refrigerator.

Suleiman could not have been more than thirty years old. He was short and inclined to plumpness, wore a double-breasted European suit and an ivory Sufi rosary around his neck. On his left hand there was a lozenge-shaped turquoise set in a massive silver ring. He looked more like a Turk, a Circassian one, than an Egyptian. His features were strongly European, and his complexion was pink-and-white.

He asked me what he could do for me, evidently only having heard that I was coming and that he should make me welcome. I said that I was interested in the Sufis, and that I wanted to know as much as possible about them before modernism erased too many of their traces.

He laughed. 'The old traces are all but erased – if by them you mean the wandering religious mendicants, the sheikhs of the Orders driving their carriages over the bodies of prostrate dervishes, that kind of thing.'

As the car sped towards Suleiman's surburban home, I asked what the 'traces' might have had to do with Sufism, or the essence of it. 'Nothing at all, for today' he said; 'once those practices had value, and that was why they were carried out. But who, today, would insist upon a metal bucket, when a plastic one is cheaper and easier to use?'

But there were still some of the old-fashioned monasteries and so forth to be found?

'Plenty. There is the Kaygusuz Haji Bektash monastery, there are the congregations of the Rifa'i, the Qadiri, the Saadi and others. But these places and many of their people, are relics. Relics have some value : some relics . . .'

Three lorry-loads of workers from the High Dam, decorated with slogans and crying for 'Arab Socialism' hurtled past us.

'What do you feel about Gamal Abdel Nasser's Egypt?' I asked the Bey.

'We have no interest in politics, if that is what you mean' he said, 'but we work with whatever constructive and desirable tendency there is wherever it may be found. Don't you do the same?'

Suleiman's house was a very fine Victorian building, standing beside a stream, surrounded by a high wall and with a garden which must have covered several acres. Numerous gardeners were supervising the watering of billiard-table turf as we swept through the wrought-iron gates.

Suleiman took me to his library, an enormous room completely lined on three walls with books, most of them in Oriental languages. The fourth wall was almost all glass, and looked out upon a fountain set in a rose-garden.

In his rather hesitant but quite good English, my host began to explain to me some of the characteristics of Sufi life. His approach was much more academic than many Sufis I had met, but he was so obviously a man of culture and wide reading that I felt that I could rely upon his information, and took as many notes as possible.

'I inherited this library and this interest, if you can call it that, from my father Hussein Kamil Bey. I might be called the historian of the Sufis here, if it were not that we use history only to illustrate points, not to form a movement.'

I asked him about the origins of Sufism.

'The School called *The Masters* (al-Khwagagan) stands behind all Sufi manifestations. This gave rise, in historical times, to organisations which have been called Orders. Like your Western monastic communities.

'One of the great teachers of this School was Bahauddin Naqshband, of Bokhara. He died in 1389. It was he who restored the basic teaching of "Zaman – Makan – Ikhwan" (Time, Place and Brotherhood). The publicly-known portion of the Masters, since his death, have called themselves Naqshbandis, after Bahauddin's surname. This name means "Masters of the Diagram", but is usually translated as "The Painters" or "Designers", like you have the "Masons" in the West; and we have

153

them, too, founded by the "Builder" Dhu'noun the Egyptian.'

What were the books of this semi-secret group?

'In addition to the best-known book – *Drops from the Fount of Life* – there is what might be called an instruction manual called *The Book of Wisdom,* issued in parts.

I asked Suleiman about the *Mu'assissa* of which the Sheikh of Kuwait had spoken, the 'Sufi Foundation'.

He looked very straight at me, as if I had said something improper.

'This is a very complicated question. History, you see, has been written by the wrong people, as often as not. This means that when we speak of good things, people think that they are bad: because the bias of the historian was against this or that subject.'

I begged him to tell me more.

'Well, this much you can know, for it is no secret, only unknown to people in general. The *Mu'assissa* was founded in Egypt, by the Fatimites, descendants of the Prophet and heirs to the inner teaching, the *Ilm el-Batini.*

It was a school and also the repository of the high knowledge, the knowledge of man.

'The Egyptian Fatimites deteriorated and were eventually overcome by Saladin. But not before they had appointed a secret institution, the Imamate, to go into hiding and operate the high knowledge's work in a secret manner.

'In order to maintain their inviolability, the headquarters of this organisation pretended to be a centre of horrors, and deliberately circulated the elaborate story that it was an assassination movement. This was the beginning of the 'sect' known as the Assassins, or the Hashishin.

'They chose this name because it resembled the real name *Asasiyin* (those of the source), and because it was very close to those whom you in the West call the Essenes of Palestine.'

I had heard, of coure, of the dreaded assassins, from whose sect the word in English is derived, and I pressed Suleiman for more details. He went on:

'Hasan, son of Sabah, the so-called Old Man of the Mountain, was playing a double game. By creating an aura of terror, he was able to wield power and preserve the community at a time when it was threatened, in Persia and Syria, from all sides.

No actual assassinations were ever carried out.'

But how did the movement get such a terrible name that everyone at that time, and since, believed that it was a terrorist and political movement?

'Quite simple. Money spreads rumour. So does fear. Whenever anyone was killed in the Middle East, and people often were murdered, if he was sufficiently important, Hasan's people would spread the word that the Assassins had done it.'

If this is true, I thought, it throws important light on a baffling page of Eastern history. I said 'If you told that to most people, they would think that you were an Ismaili trying to "improve the image" of your forbears.'

Suleiman laughed 'You can believe what you like. The real fact is that this system, call it what you will, was most concerned about saving the most important knowledge available to man. This method was a masterstroke.'

But the community which believed in the Assassin creed still existed, I protested. They had their leaders, their followers. Did *they* know this? He smiled.

'Few of them know. There is something even more important that even fewer of them know. It is this: the Agha-Khans, the leaders of this sect, those who have been publicly known in the past, they are nominees. They are what you would call in English "caretakers". They serve as a rallying-point, known as a *Hijab* (veil) awaiting the reurn of the true imam. But the true imam is always here. He is the working imam, the descendant and successor of Mohammed the Prophet.'

Then, I wanted to know, what was the purpose of the Ismaili organisation? Did it covertly co-operate with the Sufi imam, because I assumed that the current imam was a dervish?

'You do think in a tiresomely Western manner' complained Suleiman, 'the plan of the *Mu'assissa* extends beyond ordinary time. This means that the community, its leadership, its activities remain in being. But this community, its resources, its leaders, are in reserve, as it were. They are waiting until the Imam declares himself to them, so that they can carry out his bidding.'

'Do you mean that Sufis know who this Imam is and that his own community, the people who venerate his substitute, do not?'

'That is exactly what I do mean. Who ever said that the

community should know all the time who their real leader is? Surely it is more important for them to know who he is when he needs them, when he declares himself to them? What is the purpose of his being publicly known? To bask in publicity?'

Suleiman was right. This was a cenception far too Eastern for my mind to take in fast.

'But,' I protested, 'if this process has been going on for some time, and I assume that the whole Ismaili community has been in moth-balls for generations, how in the name of all that is good can we be sure that they, or some of them, or their leaders, will in fact recognise the true imam when he does appear?'

'There are provisions for that,' said Suleiman. 'The first provision is that the legend that there are *Hijabs* has been passed down in their scriptures. That may or may not die out. Secondly, there is word of mouth teaching from one *Hijab* to another. That, too, might die out, because an usurping *Hijab* might not want to surrender the throne. Then, last of all, there is the "guidance". This is a method whereby all imams and leaders of the Ismailis must pray – call it on a certain wavelength – for guidance in vexed questions. If and when the real imam wanted to present himself to the existing Ismailis, he would do so at first indirectly, but with a challenge to their equanimity which would cause them to pray in a certain manner, for guidance. This would bring them onto the wavelength. They would contact the "message" left for them hundreds of years ago, the message about the true imam.'

I was curious to know more about this 'wavelength' which defied time and space, and which contained a 'deposit' of information which could be called almost at will.

'There is little I can tell you about it,' was all that Suleiman would say, 'except that one teaches the other how to pray for guidance. When the question is in his mind, the suppliant, big or small, will pray. Little by little the fact of the existence of the true imam will come to him. Then he gets in touch with him.'

I had to say that of all the wonderful things I had heard since making contact with Sufis, this was the one most like a fairy-tale.

'Fairy-tales are true, if you know their meaning.'

Before I left, Suleiman gave me three objects. The first was a large piece of Bokharan embroidery, with flowers of nine petals each on a maroon ground. The second was a small ring, probably silver, with a turquoise set into the bezel. The third was a phial of yellowish powder. 'Add water to it, and you have a colouring matter' he said.

I had absolutely no idea as to what possible use these items might be to me, or to anyone else, for the matter He soon told me. 'People often talk about magical objects, in fairytales and folklore' he said. 'These are not magical, but they belong to *another* realm of human action and thought. I will try to explain. If you use a certain colour, and certain textures, to decorate your room, your living-space, they may have a certain effect upon you. This is well known to modern psychology. Again, if you have a certain kind of temperament, you will tend to surround yourself with certain objects which correspond to it. You might decorate your room red if you were a choleric type, for instance.

'But there is another *range* of environmental effects. The ancients knew them. This tapestry is not only the product of a certain kind of thought, but it is a *pattern* of it. It could communicate with the equivalent in your mind. The same with the other objects. It is this knowledge, and no mere superstition, which is the foundation for the folklore beliefs.'

But could I simply surround myself with certain objects, survivals from an antique knowledge, and let them work on me? No, apparently it was not as simple as that.

'You will have to find someone who can unlock the inner content of these materials for you. Just the same as if you had a transistorised radio set and had to find a battery to connect to it. Knowledge works in the same way as matter. It must be aligned in a certain way. But do not despise the vehicle: it is all you have got at the moment.'

CHAPTER FOURTEEN

The Secret of the Teachers

We in the West are very accustomed to being told that we do not understand spirituality, or that the East is the repository of ancient secrets; that we are materialistic and have to slough off the accretions of centuries of inattention to 'real values' – and so on.

This kind of talk I heard from the Sufis among whom I lived and whose lives I shared. But it was not quite put in the same way as I had heard before. And that was what gave me the opportunity to try to determine exactly what it meant.

It really took nearly three years before I realised that the purpose of reproach about the 'lack of spirituality' was not designed to make one feel ashamed, to make greater efforts, to dedicate oneself to the service of the people putting the point of view. This discovery was almost alarming. I use this word because, when I understood what the Sufis were talking about, I also realised how their doctrine, one of real spirituality, had deteriorated in the hands of repetitionists. Take the Indian Sadhu, who practises renunciation of the 'things of the world'. There can be little doubt that originally such Sadhus lived a certain kind of life for a certain period of time, in order to acquire a different viewpoint on life. Then the means became an end; and it is easy to see how rapidly and completely this can take place. A teacher tells a disciple to restrain himself from this or that. Taking the teaching literally, the disciple himself, unless under constant guidance, will reason, consciously or otherwise: 'If a certain amount of restraint is useful, then complete restraint will surely take me to the very end.'

Going over the teachings of the New Testament from this point of view I could immediately grasp that this, and nothing else, was the reason for the apparently contradictory teachings of Jesus, of which so much has been made. Jesus was teaching. He was addressing one group of people at one time, another at another. He was, in the Sufi manner, 'prescribing' this or that technique for this or that person. But, through misunderstanding, greed, ignorance of the system as a whole, the hearers or their successors lumped the whole tradition together, with the result that it appears to critical minds to be chaos.

This discovery, or realisation, made such an amazing impact upon my mind that I felt a sudden and overmastering re-attraction towards Christianity, what it was trying to do; towards the Founder of the Faith. I could see, as if reflected in a mirror, the efforts of two thousand years of well-meaning people trying to apply esoteric and spiritual principles mechanically. Again and again the dictum, whether conscious or unconscious : 'If it is good for one person, it must be good for all.' And, again, the belief : 'If a little of this is good, a lot must be so much better.'

I realised, too, even before the Shah pointed it out to me, that this process, this deterioration of teaching, was as much a problem in the East as in the West. In fact, the process had gone to a far greater extent in the East, partly because the East had a longer history of teaching, at any rate recorded, and that the message or Buddha or Zoroaster or even Confucius, had obeyed the natural law that it would 'run down' even before Christianity.

It was with thoughts of this kind that I left Cairo to visit Baghdad, the ancient home of the Sufis where many of the classical masters lived, taught and died. I was on my way, too, to sit at the feet of Idries Shah, who was spending some time in the city.

He was the guest of a member of an ancient and influential family, whom recent political disturbances had not succeeded in dislodging from his beautiful palace.

As I entered the reception-room the Shah at once got up, seated me beside him, offered me a cigarette, and started to talk as if we had never been parted.

I tried to look at him and hear his words in a different way from the first time, in Damascus. The atmosphere around a man, often produced by the way in which people react to him, can produce a false judgment. I had come with questions, and to try to assess more : but this time the questions were very different from the first time, and the assessment was somehow of a different kind.

I was not very surprised when he answered all my questions before they were asked. I only said : 'You are answering unspoken questions, which are in my mind. But I would like to know, if I may, if you deliberately set out to affront or discourage people by what might be called dissimulation. Do you, in fact, make people think that you are not what you really are, in order to get rid of them?'

'My dear fellow' he said at once, 'What possibly better way could there be? You are right. You see, if you try to persuade someone of the truth of what you are saying, you may succeed or you may not. If you succeed, you may have succeeded only in inducing belief, not in communicating usefulness. If you do not succeed, you might as well get rid of the person. If you make them think that you are useless to them, this is kinder than making them think that they have not "passed a test" or anything like that.'

'Then what are you seeking in people?'

'Capacity to *be,* to serve, to understand. Not belief that they believe.'

It was by a series of points given to me on this occasion that I learned the Sufi answer to a myriad problems about the so-called secret teaching in esotericism.

Much of it was entirely new to me, some of it I was beginning to suspect but could not have formulated so precisely. I honestly believed and do believe that this is the hidden knowledge for which people search – in the wrong places.

Summarised, the teaching claims that there are very few people at any given time on earth in a position to understand what man's position really is for that epoch. Such people sometimes have a teaching mission, sometimes not. If they are of the latter type, they have some sort of mission which they discharge in mysterious ways. If they have a teaching this mission has to be carried out as and when, and where, it *can* be carried out. It is not like a doctor, say, who – once trained – puts up his plate, gains a reputation and attracts patients.

The true teacher is a part of a team. He may be the head of it, but he depends upon his associates for carrying out the total activity known as the Teaching, perhaps in many parts of the world at once. If a man has to learn something, then, he may have to pass from one expert to another, in order to develop the necessary constellation of capacities. His instructors may or may not be 'teachers'.

This whole concept is so eminently possible, and yet so foreign to the primitive thinking which states that a teacher must know everything and pass it all on in measured doses, that when I first heard it I was flabbergasted. It bore the stamp of truth, for me at least. Why ever had I never thought of it before?

All kinds of things began to fall into place. This was the answer to why Jesus, for instance, did this and did not do that. The answer to the question why people on the spiritual path, in all kinds of disciplines, literally had to 'travel' here and there. The answer why institutionalised teaching of wisdom always deteriorated, in spite of the high calibre of the teachers: because the possibility of a total teaching, made up of many, many facets, did not exist.

The beauty and hugeness, grandeur and possibility, hope for mankind of such a widespread and knowing teaching suffused my being.

Here at last was something in which a twentieth-century man could believe about a 'hidden teaching', without becoming a credulous dupe of some kind of system which merely appealed to primitive feelings of fear or covetousness, of personality-worship, of local religion. This was what everyone among my Sufi friends, whatever their breed (Buddhist, Hindu, Moslem, Christian) referred to as the High Teaching and the Dervish Work.

And because so much of this is to be found in the New Testament, because the dervishes revere Jesus so much, this was the reason that they were slightingly called 'only Christians' by the fanatics and atheists who had heard something of what they said and did.

This was the secret of the teacher. Where the unregenerate man or woman looked for the teaching in books, it resided in individuals, who 'operated' it, as the Masons might say. Where institutions believed that they could preserve it, it was impossible to institutionalise. Where people looked for a single, individual, source of knowledge, it was diffused among mankind. Those who knew the patterns of its diffusion were helping in this effort The rest, like the blind men of the fable, were fumbling with pieces of it.

The secret of the teacher was that he taught his students just what he could and what was necessary. Then he directed them to study on their own, or to travel to another teacher, for a definite and understood purpose. Such a man would have to be very different from the mahatmas adopted by a desperate humanity, anxious to find 'all truth under one roof' as if it were a department store.

Such a teacher would have to be very different from the mystical teacher who insisted upon keeping his disciples forever around him and dependent upon him. He would have to be free of any vestige of 'self'.

Reading the Sufi classics I realised that this was the 'Ancient and Guide' about whom so many of the ancient masters had been speaking.

I could have no doubt that Idries Shah was such a man.

I said all this to him. He said: '*You* may understand all this, but it will not be likely to survive one remove. By this I mean that if you try to communicate it, you will either be laughed at or misunderstood. People will either accept this idea, and drag it down to idolatry; or else they will reject it, thinking that you are just another obsessed individual peddling a cult into which you have somehow been indoctrinated.'

I said: 'Then what is one to do?'

He answered: 'Those who can hear properly, will hear. Those who can see rightly, will see. The rest will twist everything and those are the people whom we call "primitive" and for whose sake we are really working. Like the man in the jungle who is trying to teach hygiene to the savages, we are trying to lay down a basis of rational and proper understanding of mysticism. At the same time we are carrying out the Higher Task. Address yourself to those who may be prepared to learn and teach the bases (the equivalent of boiling utensils to sterilise them) not those attracted by the Higher Task (equivalent to becoming a master surgeon in one leap).

I vowed that if it were given to me, I would try to do so.

The Shah dismissed me and said that I should not return to my Afghan friends. I took the bus to Basra, en route for Bombay, where I would take an aircraft for the short trip to Karachi, to see some friends and attend to small matters of business. Then I would be free to make for Kunji Zagh once more.

CHAPTER FIFTEEN

Basra to Bombay

I took ship from Basra to Bombay in company with three disciples of the Shah. Because they regarded themselves as engaged upon a private mission, I am constrained to respect their request to 'subdue their identity' as it was put to me. I would not have mentioned them at all were it not for the fact that the mosiac of their accounts of the nature, purpose and manner of proceeding of Sufism today presented me with a wholly remarkable picture of an undertaking only faintly glimpsed by most Western observers.

I shall call them Wahid, Ithnen and Thalatha. Wahid was grey-haired, British, a retired optician who had practised in Britain, Australia and in the Army. He had none of the tiresome mannerisms of people who embrace odd cults and try to conceal their interest or else make a convert at all costs. His manner could best be described as courtly. I estimate him at about sixty-five years of age.

Ithnen was Finnish, aged about forty, looked younger, spent five months of the year as a cruise-captain mainly in the Mediterranean, and was remarkably fluent in English. Thalatha was an earnest young American, with no profession that I could discover. His parents had been Russians, and he had been attracted to the Sufis through his reading about a certain emigré couple, Gurdjieff and Ouspensky, who had tried to systematise and convey certain Sufi teachings in the West between the two world wars.

These three were unusually forthcoming about the place of Sufism in metaphysics, in history and in their own lives. This may have been intended by the Shah, or it may have been that their background was Western, and that they still retained a good deal of the intellectual objectivity which was their birthright.

Since I kept notes only immediately after each conversation, and took no current shorthand note, I will not attempt to reconstruct dialogue. What follows, however, is the exact substance of question-and-answer exchanges after which I retired to my cabin and summarised points which I had made sure were correct.

Ihnen, as we paced the deck of the little British-Indian ship, gave me the first really important argument. I had been saying that it was extremely hard to make a coherent picture of the activities and scope of the Sufi effort. I used the word 'effort' because I did not even know what rightly to call it.

I expected the usual circuitous answer. Instead, he looked straight into my eyes and said that a straight question called for a straight answer. I told him that I always hoped that it did.

Ithnen now said that Sufism was known as Tasawwuf to its practitioners. This was a code-phrase for another term, which meant Divine Wisdom, Hikmet al-ilahi. This was the name given to the ancient science, originating from somewhere beyond our usual time-space conception. This science was operated by a basic group of Supreme Adepts. They had always existed, in a certain way. Their representatives still existed and always would.

Their task was to keep a sort of censorship of the psychic currents of man. In accordance with how these currents waxed and waned, they supplied more fuel from a source which they controlled.

I asked them how they did it.

It was done in many ways. Basically, however, these people caused, by a sort of remote control, a current of energy to rise and fall. This, as a secondary manifestation, gave rise to what we know as religions.

Did he mean that all outer religious forms were in fact *projections* of a deeper meaning which had a terrestrial origin?

This was exactly what he meant.

Then there were intermediaries, people who played no visible part in events, who in fact inspired others to become religious teachers on earth?

That was so.

Wahid, at a slightly later conversation, told me something about how these people are supposed to operate, according to Sufi doctrine. In the first place the consciousness of the Sufi 'work' resides within the whole community. This means that the Sufis are to be looked upon as one whole: a community of people who act as a sort of electrical battery which accumulates and discharges a certain sort of energy essential for human progress. This progress, however, is evolutionary : it leads towards the growth of a higher form of man. All other human enterprises are less important sometimes these other enterprises (some of which we prize so much, as nations, cultural groupings and so on) have to be attenuated because they are producing a force hostile to real human growth.

This must surely mean, I objected, that there is a form of super-human being, a product, already in being?

Wahid gravely assured me that this was true. This being, known by many other names in other cults, was that which was really directing the development of man.

I realised that this might be true, but complained that to think of all human enterprises as second-class and ultimately under the control of superman was repugnant to most people's thinking.

Wahid assured me that this was so, and that the only person who could see the importance of this was he who had seen or felt the process at work. I asked him to amplify.

These words I took down verbatim :

'If all human effort is slightly misguided; that is to say incorrect because it is based on grouping, a real human being with his own and his race's welfare at heart would like to see the true pattern, so that he could harmonise with what is best for the emergence of a real, progressive, free man.'

'Yes, but how can a person have demonstrated to him the truth of what you say? He could never accept what you just said as an article of faith. He might merely be insane, or obsessed by a cult which claimed supremacy over every man on earth.'

'You are quite right. This means that a certain number of human beings who can be useful to this supreme effort have to be enabled to see the truth of it as a matter of experience? Don't you yet understand that this is what the Sufis are doing when they increase their numbers? Not the numbers of their credulous followers. But the numbers of those who can see what is going on, can be trusted with the knowledge, and who can be useful to this holy task.'

I took a deep breath, because this was something almost impossible to grasp.

Wahid did not say any more on this subject, and I completed the story from a conversation with Thalatha.

First I wanted to know, how could a convincing and objectively satisfying proof be shown that such a process as that alleged actually did exist?

The answer was that there *is* a way; and that way is shown to those who are worthy. Why only those? The answer seemed logical enough:

The Way is shown to those who can understand and who can contribute, and who can *attain*. As with any other specialisation, there was no point, and little possibility, of showing it to anyone else. Thalatha reminded me that you might describe the miracle of a grub becoming a butterfly to a savage. But if you were a third-year teacher of biology it would be inappropriate, inefficient and breaking your contract to try to teach its meaning to that savage.

I said that this sounded very high-handed to me.

So, too, said Thalatha, would we sound to a savage who demanded to know about butterflies when what he really needed to know was hygiene or literacy or how to grow a maize patch.

But how could a group of men arrogate to themselves such powers, by what right?

Suddenly he looked very grave. His eyes pleaded with me, as if there were unspoken words which he dared not say.

By the same right, it appeared, as any other science. There was a training-system, a body of tested materials, a corps of teachers, a task to be performed. If this science was not made available to the ordinary man, this was something that all specialisation understood.

This, he said, was as far as he could go.

We had reached an impasse. Aware of the untrustworthiness of ordinary senses, I had not relied upon them to evaluate Sufism. I had destroyed almost all my notes which dealt with what seemed to be super-natural experiences. I had refused to allow myself to believe that Sufis had in fact demonstrated miracles to me because they had themselves assured me that what was 'a miracle to one man was a commonplace to a man of greater knowledge'. Hence it could not be used as a proof of anything.

I realised, as Sufi teachers warned again and again, that

conversion to a religion or a cult was a simple matter which could be 'engineered', and that the inner conviction that this or that was true did not prove anything. In this I had confirmation from the work of Western medical men who in the past few years had exposed the mechanism of brainwashing and religious conversion. I had also met many men and women who faithfully and as they thought honestly held opposite views in politics, religion, even science.

Now I was excluded from understanding something that I desperately wanted to understand because there was an invisible but definite barrier. I realised that if there was a true spiritual quest the would-be student could only go so far.

It was for *them* to accept or reject my candidature. No amount of formal knowledge, no quantity of effort, could do more for me.

When we docked at Bombay, I asked Wahid to explain, if he would, one more mystery.

'Willingly, if I can.'

'When I asked Idries Shah to help me with a whole range of my problems, he told me to do some very strange things. He said that I was to find a stone with green flecks on it, was to keep this with me for a certain number of days, was to recite certain formulae, and to try to project my mind towards what I thought was right. I carried out these things, though they had no logic I could see. In ten days all my physical and financial problems had cleared up. How did this work?'

'More easily than you think. There is a hidden correspondence between things of the world and things of a second system of progress. Having satisfied himself that it would be permissible to intervene in your affairs, he told you about the things – some material, some connected with your own mental orientation – which would solve them. This is all that happened. People who know what is *really* going on in the world *can* intervene in the mechanism.'

'But how does this affect their working on their own plan? Surely my affairs cannot be important enough for Idries Shah to suspend his own activities – if I am right in assuming that he is the Master, or one of the Masters who maintain the progress towards higher evolution?'

'When you are operating in that range you can do many

things which accord both with your needs and the welfare of others. This is something which is difficult to describe. But let me say this : that if it had been desirable for the general plan for you to be benefited in another way, you would have been given different formulae, different things to do and think.'

CHAPTER SIXTEEN

Amu Daria – the River Oxus

I rendezvoused with my old friend Mirza and three young 'Seekers' at a prearranged spot, well away from the Pakistan-Afghan borderline. Mirza had given me a complete *Mullah's* outfit to put on: baggy trousers, a very long shirt, the tail extending beyond the knees, worn outside the trousers; an undershirt, scarf, diminutive turban, cummerbund, and *chapli* sandals. All of these were used, and the white shirt looked as if it had once been dipped, for the merest fraction of a second, in pale blue dye. A huge blanket completed the rigout, being placed on the shoulders and then one end whipped over the left shoulder. Thus prepared, with a small amber rosary in my hand, I rehearsed various expressions (mostly scowling) before my bedroom mirror in Karachi.

I was obviously not supposed to be a completely out-of-this-world Moslem ecclesiastic, in that although I had a fairly good beard I also wore a wristwatch and a pair of socks. In my sack, which was carried over one shoulder, I had a selection of necessary items. A cheap compass was for determining the direction of Mecca for prayers, a small amulet tied in a piece of red cloth was a relic of some pilgrimage to a shrine. A well-used copy of the Koran, lithographed in India, was carefully folded inside a large bandana handkerchief. There were also supplied a bag of pine-kernel nuts in a coarse cotton bag, a pair of scissors, a toothstick and a few other odds and ends.

I had no writing materials, because I was almost incommunicado. This was a *mullah* who was on the verge of Sufihood. In order to discover, by established religious practise, whether I was to enter the company of the dervishes as a member, I had taken a vow. This story was to protect me against too much conversation. The vow that I had taken was to repeat certain formulae an illimitable number of times, in accordance with the instructions given in a very famous book of magico-religious practices,

the *Jawahiri Khamsa* (Five Jewels) which may have been heterodox but was nevertheless held in a sort of sneaking regard by
very many people.

Mirza's idea to make me a sort of expert on this book was a
very fine one from the point of view of helping one's free progress into and through the Afghan-Pakistan borderland and
beyond. Many versions of the book exist, almost all of them
being in Persian, but some are in Urdu. They are invariably
lithographed, not very well, on rather indifferent paper. Since
the entire work is ultimately derived from the medieval Arab
works of the Moroccan Al-Buni and the Arab Ibn al-Hajj, some
people spend years collating their own copies, in the hope that
the mixture of magical processes and religious formulae will
yield the results which the Moorish magicians are positively
known to them (through stories at any rate) to have achieved.

The book's reputation rubs off, as it were, onto people who are
students of it. Not everyone wants the name of being a dabbler
in the occult, and hence the experts on the Five Jewels are not
often met with or will not admit to their secret vice in public.
Mirza remembered a man who gained and sustained an enormous reputation for years through his reputed mastership of the
Jewels. So I was appointed to the rank of follower of this
marvellous treasure.

Not everyone in India, Pakistan, the Pathan land and Afghanistan knew or understood Sufis. The natives of these countries
might often be against one another. But who had not heard of
the marvellous Book of the Five Jewels? Whoever had not would
soon have his ignorance repaired by information supplied by
some at least in any average crowd.

So my role boiled down in the main to acting as though I was
a semi-magician in a semi-trance, accompanying (or being accompanied by) companions with similar and Sufi interests. The
only phrase I really needed to know, in answer to a question was
'*Qasam Khurdum*' (I have taken a vow). In tricky situations it
would be up to the rest of the party to get me out. My knowledge of Persian was good enough to understand most of the
things that were being said, and that should help in planning
my reactions.

Mirza told me as soon as I arrived at the caravanserai and
introduced me to his friends, that we were not going through

the ordinary routes. We would merely stray across the border by night, and take our chance: a very good chance indeed, of being able merely to walk across without meeting anyone at all. I doubted whether any of our party had ever seen a passport, and everyone seemed equally anxious to avoid official contacts. The three Seekers were very completely under Mirza's orders, and not for one moment did I gain the impression that they thought me to be anyone unusual in their midst.

We were just over ten miles from the border, at a spot chosen to coincide with other routes further along the road. This meant that, as far as anyone knew, we had taken the right-hand fork instead of going straight ahead, and had headed back into Pakistan after visiting a small shrine which occurred conveniently by the wayside. This would be the explanation of our movements if by any chance anyone asked about us. I thought at first that it was intended to deceive the owner of the teahouse in the caravanserai, but was soon undeceived. As we sat reclining in a bare room, our backs against the wall, padded only by our bundles and waiting for evening, Mirza called the proprietor in to have tea with us.

'How much money have you with you, Mullah Saheb?' I stopped muttering my *wazifa* and scowled. I was not sure what he meant, but took out the twenty-five hundred rupees which I had brought with me, and handed the bundle to him. He gave it to the other man, to my dismay, for this was quite a large sum of money – £250. 'We collect it on the Other Side,' he told me. The proprietor placed his hand on his heart. No receipt, no counting of money. This was the way to do one's banking – if it worked.

No details, as they say in some circles, are available of the precise course which we took after that, until we found ourselves on the Other Side, heading for the first of the settlements of the Sufis which were named after a Central Asian river. But more of them in a moment. There was one incident. An army lorry with desert tyres crunched up to us as soon as we had left the road that night, to strike across a fairly bare patch of hard sand in an area where we should not have been. Before the headlamps had properly picked us up, Mirza and his companions were circling round in a frenzied dance, hooting and cheering like anyone's idea of a dervish. Taken by surprise, I froze in their midst. The driver pulled up beside us, then drove off, shouting : *pagal log* – madmen.

Amu Daria is, of course, the name of the immense river which forms four hundred miles of the northern frontier of Afghanistan beyond it lies the Soviet Union and the lost territories of Turkestan, once the site of ancient Sufi strongholds. Russian penetration into the Central Asian khanates is no new thing, and faced with the encroachment of the 'west' in the form of Czarist advance, and the need to develop Sufi teachings further in order to coincide in some way with modern technology – the Sufis started to move into the hinterland of Afghanistan during the early part of this century. Some of the oldest foundations were already established in the Hindu Kush area. Those who migrated into Afghanistan began to use the name of Amu Daria, run into one word, as the designation of their teaching. Thus they perpetuated the crossing of the river and the tradition of their trans-Oxus origins in their name.

The River Amu (Amu Daria in Persian) appears on most maps as the Oxus. It will be convenient to refer to the emigré Sufi groups as *Amuaria* ones, because such a phrase as 'the Oxus Sufis' does not sound anything like as felicitous. They are also know as the *Samoun* (a code-word for 'bee', a reference to one of their exercises).

Although the Sufis do not like to engage in historical or geographical discussions of their cult, there seems little doubt that the Amudaria elements concentrate upon practises and ideas which differ from those found elsewhere, with the exception of the old Afghan Orders. In some ways their rituals and methods are quite like those of other Sufi Orders, but more organised. As an example the habit of compiling multiple words taken from the syllables of other words is a fine art with them. The concentration upon the belief that the Sufi way is the only suitable one for propagation throughout the world is another characteristic. Then there is the teaching that it is from here that the Sufi message must be diffused, and that it will have to be naturalised in each community.

I spent one week in each of four Amudaria communities. The organisation of the monastery, according to this group, is ultimately a spiritual entity : the building or the location is secondary. Thus two of the 'monasteries' actually had no premises of their own. Meetings were held in the open, or in houses. In one village when the gun which marks noon was fired, virtually the whole population started repeating formulae under their breaths. This was a 'meeting' of the Amudarists: no monastery, not even a physical meeting.

This principle is carried even further in Afghanistan. Although monasteries exist and *halka* meetings are held, and discipleship as I had seen it elsewhere was carried on, the whole community is considered to be in a special kind of *rapport*. This means that the constant spiritual communication between the members is thought to continue, especially at designated times.

The four leaders of the trans-Oxus communities, Sheikh Jalal, Ahmad Baba, Ishan Ali and Pir Turki, all accepted the authority of the Naqshbandi chief of the Hindu Kush Sufis. This is the representative of the Studious King, who is the overall leader, and who may be 'found in disguise, in almost any country of the world'.

Ahmed Baba showed me the method of sewing the patchwork cloak which some Sufis wear, and which was until quite recently the uniform of those who were going through a period of retreat from the world. It is not known when this custom started, but I was reminded of the 'coat of many colours' and wondered whether the robe originated in Syria. Ahmad was about seventy years of age, but might have been older. He was in astonishing health for a man who could clearly remember pre-Revolution Russia, and attributed this to his carrying out the longevity exercises which are a part of Sufi training. 'Nobody,' he said 'would get feeble if he carried them out regularly. Certainly they would live, as the Sheikhs of our Order do, up to a hundred or twice as many years of age.'

In addition to most of the usual Sufi exercises, the Baba's community practised healing, and Sufis came from various places to receive this part of their 'enlightenment'. 'Of course,' said the sage, 'we can also send it out to those who are ready to receive it. You see, we only have a portion. It is like having a *karez* (underground water channel) connected to the source. But we cannot transmit to those who are not ready. If they are only slightly developed in the requisite ways, then they must come here.'

I was interested to know what these Sufis felt about the

possibility of making their cult known in the West. Ahmad was not to be drawn. 'That is a matter for the Studious King.'

Ishan Ali was a Turk, and half the age of the Baba. His ministry extended through the wild north-east of Afghanistan, right up to the Chinese border in the thin tongue of land which sits astride the Pamir mountains. He was forthright, greatly loved, and yet difficult to approach. He received me in a Western-type suit, with a small karakul lambskin hat on his shaven head, something like a kalpak cap, but more stylish. 'You must not force the pace,' he told me so many times. 'You are anxious to learn a great deal of things about us. That is good enough, and there is sufficient reason to tell you. But you must remember that if you allow yourself to be blinded by curiosity, by the collecting of facts and little snippets of information – you may write a good book, but you will slow down your spiritual progress.'

I saw him apply this teaching to a party of young men, not long out of the Army, who had come on a pilgrimage to meet him. 'Remember what I say,' he admonished them, 'for you will not be told again, but sent home. What you have learned in the Army will be of inestimable value to you, although you are still cursing the day the *pishk* (conscription) caught you, and blessing the day you were discharged. Both are wrong: but I cannot expect you to understand this yet. Pay attention to everything that you are told, and do not take an interest in things that you are not told or shown. At your stage your so-called human abilities can often be a curse to you. Plenty of time for changing back when you get to the outside world again.'

Pir Turki, who in spite of his name was not a Turk but of Indian extraction, ran the strangest school of all. Everything was based upon gymnastics. Pits had been dug in the circle which had been marked out around his miniature castle. In these depressions, some twelve feet deep, disciples had to wield heavy clubs, often to music, sometimes accompanied by the voice of the teacher. They were reputed to develop occult powers; and I heard many tales about how they could make things float on water, see at a vast distance, and so on.

It was said by local villagers that one of Pir Turki's teachers had, by the power of his glance, held up an army for three days in the passes of the Khyber. Be that as it may, Pir Turki the ascetic was a martinet. Shunning over-eating or loose talk like the plague, he provided plenty of food for his disciples, though nobody knew where the money came from. He did not make collections. There must have been a source of his income, of course, but it was never visible. One of the first things that he said to me was : 'If you revere any man, forget him; for all that matters is the Work.'

I have never seen anyone who impressed me so much. When I told him this, he took hold of a beautiful lamp which stood on his desk-table and smashed it. 'I have destroyed a thing of beauty. Do you respect me less now? I hope so.'

Then he called a disciple, accused him of theft, and sent him to wash out the assembly-room. 'Must he suffer so that I can see that you have defects?' I asked him.

'I hope that you think that I have been unjust in making him suffer' was the answer.

Unfortunately for the lesson's permanency in my case, I learned later that the disciple who had been unjustly treated had committed some grave breach of regulations and merited punishment in any case. 'You don't understand' said a disciple, when I mentioned this; 'the lesson has sunk in where it counts. That is all that counts.'

Yet punishment was something which seemed to happen very rarely among the Sufis. I would not say that they were immune to it, but as they had been taught that personal dignity was sometimes a grave disadvantage, they were not able to suffer much through being made fun of in front of each other. Manual labour on the three farms which the community owned gave many opportunities for exercises in self-development. All the income from the farms was collected by an administrator and sent to the women's welfare association, for some reason, so the Sufis did not benefit directly. And yet the Sheikh, as I have said, did not seem short of cash.

Sheikh Jalal was a feudal-type chief, a man of towering personality within a slight and delicate frame. He lived in considerable style from the income of vast inherited flocks of some of the best sheep in the country. He smoked a little, but did not seem to eat much. He always wore similar clothes, the robes and turban which old-fashioned judges assumed in Afghanistan. He was about sixty-five years old. Although surrounded by servants and a great deal of luxury, he personally partook of it little.

When, for instance, we went out shooting and felled several hundred wild duck and grey geese, none was served at his table. The birds went as gifts to the surrounding villages.

Jalal, it was rumoured, could neither read nor write. This idea must have gained currency because he was never seen with a book or a pen. His teaching was done in the normal Sufi way: through short addresses, exercises, meditations. Going with him several times on long walks, which he embarked upon without any prior notice whatever, I realised that he spent a great deal of his time in silent communion and commemoration (called *Zikr*) and that this had become almost second nature to him. He had several sons, all of them, I believe, in the Army.

He often showed small signs of a sense of perception which is repeatedly mentioned in Sufi writings as a sign of 'saintship', but which would not have been noted except by an attentive disciple or someone else very close to him. One day, for instance, he picked up a cooking-pot and took it on a walk on which I accompanied him. Stopping at a poor small house he saluted the occupant and handed in the pot. The old woman was amazed. She said that she had just broken the earthen dish in which she cooked. Again, he handed me a box of matches when I had come out without any, in spite of the fact that I could not be sure that he realised that I had left them at home. It should be mentioned that he could not have observed that I brought none with me, for I had met him in his garden, on the way from my quarters to his.

I mentioned these small indications to him. But he would not discuss them, merely saying: 'Would you make me a saint, and rob me of the power of *becoming*?'

There were many of these little instances. Some were observed by me, others reported by disciples. It was interesting to note that among the disciples stories were never exaggerated; they would often hinge upon the smallest event. This indicated to me that many of the wilder tales current among the countryfolk and others outside Sufism were elaborations of actual happenings.

It was Sheikh Jalal that I questioned on this subject in a more general way, when I referred to the tales my mother had told me about Scottish highland and country folk being 'fey' and having insights which others did not have.

'These are normal, not abnormal developments,' he said.

'They are of no value in themselves, partly proved by the fact that the experiences seldom have practical value. For every happening of this kind that is a warning or can be turned to practical use, there are a hundred which are not of any use. Why is this? Materialists would say that it merely proves that the power is fitful, partial, something of little account. What they do not know is that these are signs. They are encouragements, they show that the recipient has a real chance of developing his "gifts". They are signs that the time has come for self-work. Most people cannot use them, because they do not know that this is the *alif* (letter A) and that the *be* (letter B) follows, until there is a *iaa* (last letter of the alphabet).'

I entertained all the four Amu Daria sheikhs at one time or another by describing to them something of the life and thinking of Europe, even going back as far as I could to the days of the Middle Ages, when the East and the West had been closer together in so many ways.

Pir Turki's reaction to this information was interesting, because it showed me that there was something in his mind on this subject. 'A century and a quarter has passed' he said, 'since the message of the Great Khan about this subject, but the work has gone on uninterruptedly.' The Great Khan was Jan-Fishan, the chief of the Hindu Kush, who was a descendant of the Prophet Mohammed, and in whose family the leadership of the Sufis is believed to reside.

'The Great Khan was the first to be in touch with the West since the time of Sultan Yusuf Saladin. He actually went to India and settled there for a time. His message, which was given out just before the War of Shah Shuja (1838) was concerned with the West. From what I have heard from you and otherwise, it is still as fresh today.'

He did not revert to the message of the Great Khan for some time, and we discussed other topics. Then he told me that the Khan had said that the West was material, had lost the force of religion. This materialism was not the materialism which we understood, but was acquisitiveness pure and simple. There would be a growth in sceptical philosophy. There would have to be a great deal of suffering in the West. 'And the rule of logic and intellect will have to become so severe that there is almost nobody who will listen to truth.'

When that happened, he said, people would start to look for truth. Then the message of the Sufis would be heard. 'But the people in the West are Christians,' I objected. 'So are we!' He turned sharply to me. 'In the West they are materialists, but of the worst possible kind. They are free, free to destroy themselves; but they should not be allowed to destroy themselves, any more than a child is allowed to do so. If I insult Jesus in a Moslem country I shall be punished by law and by the people. But you have told me that people use the name of Jesus lightly, even in swear-words in the West. Is it true?'

'It is true. But I still think that there are good people, and well-meaning ones.'

'No doubt. They will probably be considered stupid by the others. And many of them will be stupid; they will follow any-one and think that he is a prophet, because they will not be able to discriminate as to what a prophet is.'

'They are very self-critical,' I hazarded.

'Self-criticism is useless without self-work. And who is to teach them?'

I tried to turn the conversation into more illuminating chan-nels. 'Can you apply your concentration to the problem, in the way which you were telling us yesterday,' I said, 'and tell me, as one who has come from the West to learn, whether there will be a growth of a community of Sufis in Europe, strong enough to have any effect on the evolution of man?'

He did not seem to concentrate at all. 'There will.'

'And will it be led by anyone?'

'It will.'

'And will this be a Westerner?'

'It will not. It will be one who is of the East, but he will make the teaching a part of the teaching of the West, as it once was, in ancient times.'

'When will the activity start?'

'It has started, slowly. Some will come and try to force another teaching into the shape of the original one, and many will follow.'

He cut the conversation short. 'Only the Sheikhs can influence this development; it cannot be discussed. It is a matter of the contact of minds. Some who have fixed ideas may have to die to make way for someone who is younger by many years.'

Amu Daria – the River Oxus

In many ways my time with the Amudaria was the most interesting of all my life. There was something un-oriental about them; and they were so obviously intent upon some activity which was not of the rarefied nature which characterises Indian and Far Eastern thought and makes it unacceptable to any but a small minority of Westerners. There was a very great deal that one could get hold of, as it were, and very obviously no attempt at mystification.

CHAPTER SEVENTEEN

Stray Days

Khoja Imdad and I used to spend hours together, talking about our travels and discussing what might be called the lighter side of mystic life. The Khoja (master) was a wanderer, had been to Pekin and Canton, knew Malaya and Saudi-Arabia. He and my first Sufi friend, Mirza, had been travelling companions, and had been through many experiences together. Although he looked very much younger, he must have been something like eighty, for he spoke vividly of the Boxer Rebellion in China. 'There were Afghans there, you know,' he said, with the relish of an old campaigner, 'mercenaries, of course, from the cavalry Brigade of the Great Khan. The Chinese gave out that they were using magic and all kinds of sorcery. Nobody believed them. The Afghan lads bedded their horses down on dragon-painted silk, and fed them imperial honey.'

I asked him about the Sufi belief that 'a lie may be the truth', which recurs so often in the sayings of the teachers. It was all according to the point of view, he told me. People could not bear to think that they did not know the truth, therefore they concocted a truth for themselves. Therefore, taking an obvious instance, if a community believed that the Sun was a god, the man who told them it was not one would be a liar. His truth would be their lie. This theme recurred throughout the human story, whenever people tried to communicate a truth which was not already commonly accepted.

Belief, he told me, mistaken belief, generally produced suspicion. This was why narrow-minded people suspected others. This is because people who hold certain tenets, who think that they 'believe' them, can be so destructive. They want to force out of mind, out of sight, anything or anyone opposing their 'truth'.

'Of course,' he continued, 'this is an evidence that the person really knows that his 'truth' is not truth at all.'

I asked him to give me examples, and if possible to draw upon his travel experiences, for they fascinated me.

'It will have to come out in the conversation' he said. This might have been a rebuke, or it might merely be part of his way of thinking. I was not sure, so I asked him to continue and tell me more about the suspiciously-minded.

'The essentially weak man is suspicious-minded. Rumi, one of the Greatest Masters, has described him again and again. He says that when a man suspects another of trying to impose upon him, the suspicious one is looking in a mirror. He is weak and fearful, like the dog which barks but does not intend to bite.'

'But can his weakness be reduced, and his suspicion made into something healthier?'

'Only if he does two things, and he is often incapable of them. The first is that he should behave like a strong man, a man who needs not fear. The other is that he has to become happier and more balanced. The stronger man will approach with an open, understanding mind. He does not fear, and so he does not have to "bark".'

'I thought it was jealous men who opposed others, and sought to bring them down, to disgrace them.'

'Jealousy is only one part of weakness. As for disgrace, the ant cannot disgrace the elephant, though he thinks he can. An ant, meeting an elephant, may make fun of him for his bulk, and may get all other ants to do so as well. As far as the ants are concerned, the elephant is disgraced. But as far as actual truth is concerned, the ants are fools.'

'Have you ever encountered this opposition?'

'Yes, indeed. Everyone has. I went to an Indian town to teach, on the orders of my Master some half a century ago. As soon as I arrived there and visited various people, opposition to me started. The first thing that I did was to help an old woman wash clothes at the riverside. This was considered to be currying favour. Nobody else would do it, so they thought that I did it for the effect it would have on them. They were determined not to be influenced by such a simple trick as this. They did not notice that if I had stolen her laundry they would have opposed my action in the same way.'

'And what if you had remained inactive, neither washing her clothes nor stealing them?'

'I would have been just like the rest.'

'Then what happened?'

'I was becoming established as a charlatan. Deep down inside them, the people thought that all *gurus* were frauds. It was just that their local ones were people whom they feared.'

'Or people whom they did not want exposed?'

'That is the same thing, ultimately. I spoke very little Urdu at the time, therefore I could not be much more than flesh and blood. 'They say', said a merchant with whom I was passing the time of day, 'that you are only a human being, wearing the mantle of a dervish.' 'That I am,' I said, 'a human being, like all of us.'

'Not like all of us,' said the merchant, 'Guru Ganesji is a god.'

'Then what happened?'

'Then they tried to test me. People must test, you know. Take two pieces of alloy to any village imbecile anywhere and he will give you an opinion as to which one is real gold. All they could do was to try to test me by their own standards. The fisherman was trying to test the carpetmaker, as a Sufi once said.'

'I had one friend' continued the Khoja, 'a young man who from the start wanted to know whether I could teach him to read and write. I told him that I did not know his language, and that although I knew the script – which was the same as mine – I would not be sure of the spelling. They have strange sounds there which require adapted letters. But he said that anything would be better than no literacy at all. So I taught him what I could. He took what he had written to the public-letter-writer, who denounced me as a fraud, because as it happened the spelling was right. I was threatening his business, of course. More than that, I had claimed that I could not spell Urdu, and here I was doing it; trying to gain a reputation for working miracles.'

'But how did it happen that you could spell Urdu when you did not know the adapted letters they use?'

'When the need is there, the brain produces the result. This is what you call telepathy. What actually happens is that there is a contact made with the 'essence' of the language. You could not write say, Greek in this way, unless you knew something of Greek to start with, but if you knew the Greek alphabet you would be able to write in an adaptation of Greek.'

'Is this a part of mental evolution?'

'Yes, of course it is. Do you think that the ideas which people have at the same time in different places are always telepathy?

'No, they are due to like causes acting on the brain. The need produces the result. Experience is passed down from one generation to the next. A cat hunts mice, even if it has been reared without a mouse in sight. The same is true of finer qualities. There is no miracle about it, except the general miracle that we are forever evolving.'

'How did you establish yourself in India?'

'My master had told me when he sent me there only to act exactly as I felt impelled to act. If there was anything about which I was uncertain, I was to retire into contemplation until the next Thursday night. I should spend the whole night in contemplation, and then act on what was vouchsafed to me. This I did. As a result people started to say that I had an infallible intuition about things, and that the local *guru* was afraid of me. This last was because he had refused to provide someone with a charm against me.'

'Why did the *guru* do this?'

'Because he was not a bad *guru*. His instinct told him that I had a function there, and he was not selfish enough to try to maintain his position against mine.'

'But the people misinterpreted this, and thought that he was afraid?'

'I told you that people see things in the way they want to see them. They judge people by themselves. They naturally concluded that if it were *them,* they would refuse an anti-Sufi charm only if they were afraid.'

'Did you have any contact with the *guru*?'

'Eventually, yes. I went to see him and said "Guru, I have no secret which cannot be learned. I invite you to my Way. Invite me to yours, if you will". He was friendly, and there was no disagreement between us. True, he thought that he was a divine incarnation, but this was only because people had told him that he was, and the gross part of his nature accepted this possibility. We became friends. I stayed there twelve years, with just a few breaks.'

I collected stories from another Sufi, whose name I never

knew. In the usual Afghan way, he had a name and also a semi-title by which he was known. He was, to all of us, simply 'Pathani Fakir', or 'Fakir Saheb', and he referred to himself merely as 'Fakir' – one of the words which are used for a Sufi, and sometimes for an Indian – Hindu – religious mendicant. One of the interesting things about him was that he was caught in Bokhara when the Russians took it, and lived there as a Soviet worker for twenty-five years. He spoke a little Russian, but as a factory worker almost always used Persian of the slightly Iranian flavour which is spoken in this part of Soviet Asia.

He taught me the Persian words for such esoteric practises as 'over-filling a cotton quota' and what seemed to be 'crash programme' – when a thing had to be done regardless of the cost in men, materials or money. Unlike most Afghans, he was not anti-Russian, but regarded the whole of the Soviet 'experiment' – as he called it – with some amusement. 'It cannot last, you know' he would say, 'because the Russians have fallen into their own trap. They have allowed people to retain their own language, and they have encouraged local culture. They did this in the early days because they were not strong enough to Russianise everything, and because they had to have showplaces to influence the rest of Asia from. Then, even during the worst of the Stalinist terror, they had to keep up local culture even if only because Stalin was not a Russian. He was a Georgian, and he made sure everyone knew it.'

I wondered whether he was not over-optimistic, and said so, to his surprise.

'You cannot feel that way if you are actually living under the Red Flag. During the early period we were a little alarmed when the party chiefs and factory managers and all sorts of important people turned out to be Russians. But when we got to know them, we found out that they feared Moscow more than we did. That is to say, they did not like many of the aspects of Communism which were said to be necessary. This meant that they did not really accept communism, deep down. Then they learned our language, and they found that we were not savages, but had our own culture. All this influenced them very much. The "national heroes" like Ali-Sher Nawai who have been given such publicity in Soviet Central Asia are Sufis and other non-Communists.'

'What about the risings of Shamyl in Caucasia? He was supposed to be a Sufi leader, and his followers have been denounced again and again by the Russians.'

'This is what the Communists call "muridism". "Murid" as you know, means "Sufi disciple". Propaganda has swung backwards and forwards. Sometimes Shamyl is a hero, sometimes a villain. This very manipulation of the personality makes people distrust the manipulators.'

'Can a Sufi be a Communist?'

'Can a tree be a piece of cheese? They are entirely different things, and the one cannot be the other. The fanatic Communist is as vulnerable as anyone else. Because of his instability he can even swing into anti-Communist activity. This is why people have been purged so often. People think that it is because of the fear of the ruling men that they have to destroy their followers, many of whom are convinced Communists. If you had lived in the Soviet Union, you would have known that the more "Communist" a person is, the more unreliable he is likely to become. A really convinced Communist lasts only a short time; perhaps five or ten years. After that he reverts to human type again. This does not mean that he becomes better. He may become a good deal worse. He may not become capitalist-minded, but he may well become acquisitive, self-centred and dangerous to the Party. The Party needs not evil men, but willing, self-sacrificing men and women, who will keep the machine going. Every Communist goes through a phase like that, but only very abnormal people remain suitable Communists for really long periods.'

How did the Sufis operate in the Soviet Union?

They were, nowadays, mostly young. This was because the old people remained staunch Moslems, and often carried with them the worst aspects of ecclesiastical conservation. The young were discouraged by the Party from having any exchange of thought with them. During the Second World War, many young people began to feel that they needed some sort of faith. The rallying-cry to die for Mother Russia meant nothing to them, although it sufficed for the Russian troops. But a large part of the re-formed forces of the Soviet Union were composed of people from the Moslem areas.

'It was then that the Sufis got to work. Their effect was

remarkable, but understandable. These were older men who had remained aloof from the old conservatives' attempt to protect the remains of the priest-ridden religion. When younger people started to receive Sufi teaching from men whom they knew to be opposed to the scholastics, the *mullahs,* whom they had taken for sensible, progressive men, successful in their jobs, they were profoundly affected.'

The Fakir, too, had fought in the Russian Army, in the Caucasus. When he was demobilised he decided to settle in Afghanistan, where he had been as a young student. One night he took a couple of inflated ox-skins, tied them together and made what is called a *mushak,* and floated across the wide Oxus to freedom.

Shahzada (Prince) Pailuch was another companion of my free days among the highland Sufis. I never knew whether he was a real prince or not, partly because a Sufi may be called by a title which is used also in the non-Sufi world. His name, literally translated, means 'barefoot', the phrase often used to denote someone who has nothing. As a matter of fact he was generally well-dressed, and wore riding boots of the Mongol type, plus an immense *posteen,* a fur coat with embroidery outside and the fur turned inwards.

Pailuch was an Afghan through and through: which meant that he could ride, shoot, tell amusing stories, was full of self-confidence and loved nothing better than *pilao,* steaming plates or roast meat and saffron-tinted rice. He was a perfectionist. I would often meet him playing out a complicated chess-game against himself, or borrowing people's knives to sharpen because he believed that a man must be able to sharpen a knife 'ZKBT' as he called it – the initials of the phrase 'rapidly, perfectly and easily'. He was between thirty and forty, of towering height and proportions. In his face one could see several of the strains which make up the Afghan populace: Mongol, Arab, Pathan. Eyes slightly slanted, nose slightly hooked, physique enormous. From the wry stories which he told I determined that he had been in India, could cook, was fond of sports. He had once been a stoker on a British ship, but 'I had to call myself an Indian, for no Afghan could be a stoker.'

'Did you feel that this would have affected your dignity?'

'I did not have time to assess that,' he grinned, 'all the other stokers were Afghans or Pathans, and they warned me that they would not allow any foreigner to say that an Afghan was a stoker.'

'Why become a stoker?'

'Good money, travel, bad companions draw you into it.'

In America he had become a sword-swallower in rather an interesting way. He somehow got on a ship bound for the United States, and in the third-class section met a sword-swallower. When he decided to spend some French leave ashore he ran out of money somewhere, and idly noticed a circus pitching a big top in a field. So he just went to the ringmaster and offered himself as a sword-swallowing act. 'I said I was a Persian,' he said, 'because in America an Afghan means a kind of dog, the *tazi,* and because my stokers had taught me that one always had to be something else.'

His way of putting things was always amusing.

'Had you ever done any sword-swallowing before?'

'No, but that was easy.'

'You just swallowed swords, I suppose?'

'No, you see, when I was talking to the real sword-swallower on the ship, he told me two things. One was that you could get swords whose blade disappeared into the handle as you appeared to swallow them. I had no money for one of these. The other thing he said was that there was a way to do the trick, and that it was described in books. I spoke no English, really, but I got an Afghan to find a book in a public library and translate it to me. It had illustrations, too.'

'How did you find an Afghan?'

'Easier than you think.'

All Afghans have the name *khan* attached to the end of their names. Pailuch remembered someone telling him that many Afghans retained this appellation at the end of their names as a sort of surname when they went abroad. All he needed was a telephone directory of New York.

'I managed to ask someone to show me the page where the name *khan* appeared. Then I started to ring them up. If the voice which answered did not understand my language, I hung up.'

'How long did it take to find one?'

'Longer than you would think. I had eleven dimes. I had spent six of them before I realised that I would probably spend the lot before I got an answer suitable to my intentions. I thought I would try one more before I gave up.'

'And he *was* an Afghan?'

'Anything but. He asked me where I was, and I managed to tell him. Presently a man arrived, speaking only English, in a huge car. He put me in it and took me to a very sumptuous apartment, and gave me a room. He kept saying 'Israel'. Well, you know that many Pathans call themselves Beni Israel, and this was something in common between us. After half an hour an old man in a black hat arrived and started to speak to me in a strange language, which my new friends did not understand, but they smiled and nodded their heads. Then they showed me candlesticks and *khatam Daud* (the Seal of David), and still I could not understand. Finally I said 'Iran, Irani, Hind,' and words like that.

'They brought a man called Irani to see me. He spoke Persian. He explained to us all that I was not a Jew. The people I had telephoned spelt their names something like *khan*. The man I had asked to look in the telephone book thought I meant this Jewish name. When I rang the seventh number of this Hebrew succession, they thought I must be from Israel, just landed, and, brought one of their priests to speak to me in their old language. We became good friends. Irani was a Jew as well, in spite of his name, and I told them all about the Jews in Afghanistan, and they were very interested.'

'You said that it was easier than I thought to find an Afghan in New York.'

'It was easy, when you look back at it. If I had walked out of that apartment it would have been difficult. As it was all I had to do was to wait until someone understood me, saying a word or two at a time.'

'What about the circus?'

'We started to telephone all the people with Afghan names in the book. Soon I found one, who took me to his house. I had only three days to start my act, and he got me library books and an old sword. I polished it and learned. Then I became a circus act. I was sensational."

He saved enough money to return to Europe, when he discovered that he had no passport. I said that I supposed he went to the authorities in Washington and asked for one.

'We have a proverb, "Flee the Devil, but stay with him if the alternative is the government official." No, I got on a ship and got back to Bombay by degrees. Then I was all right.'

CHAPTER EIGHTEEN

Into Kafiristan

For the last three days our caravan had crept slowly through rocky defiles, swept at times by surprisingly icy blasts as we crawled along ledges which hardly seemed fit for human or even animal traffic. We were a considerable distance north-east of Kabul, capital of Afghanistan (which city we had avoided) and two days' journey from Margal, our destination. I had exchanged my Mullah blanket for a thick postin with the lambs-wool inside, buckled with an enormous belt, and put on heavy curly-toed cloglike shoes such as the Afghan peasants wear. A shaggy fur cap with ear-flaps kept my head warm.

This was the road, if road it was, to Kafiristan, heading zig-zaggedly across the ranges of the Hindu Kush, the Hindu Killer mountains, said to have been so named because a whole caravan of Indian merchants were, in some remote age, found frozen to death in a glacier. The spring snows, melting to supply the water torrents which rushed so amazingly in what seemed to be all directions, had caused avalanches which had deposited piles of stones and rubble on the ledges which so often formed our roadway. The only way to deal with them was to heave the lot out of our way, and to allow gravity to do the rest. This was likely to be dangerous for other travellers who might in their turn find the pathway blocked or even carried away, but there was no alternative, and everyone bent to the task at first with relish, then automatically, whenever it arose.

As we climbed breathing became less effective as a means of gaining oxygen. At first we did not seem to feel this strain so much, but we did notice that the going seemed heavy when it was not for the animals. Eventually we had to dismount to allow the small Qataghani ponies to make their own way, giving our own lungs extra work. It might be early Summer in the lower parts of Afghanistan, but in these uplands it was cold. Now and again we glimpsed small villages on some distant hillside, sheltered to some extent by the mountain escarpment, but baffling in the matter of just how people managed to reach them.

I discovered my first village in a very direct manner. As I was looking across a mountain-shelf, cursing the luck which had not made me a mountaineer, gazing at a very beautiful vista of a valley green with some crops and dotted with small bodies of water, I distinctly smelt woodsmoke somewhere near at hand. Yes, it was coming from below. Over the edge of what seemed to be a true precipice was a huddle of wood-built near-chalets hugging the mountain wall along whose side I was making my way behind the Sufi caravan. I felt that I could almost reach out and touch the houses, and saw three tiny children playing some sort of simple game and clapping their hands. The whole of the region, as I later discovered, was covered with these almost invisible villages. Sometimes they were built against mountain walls, sometimes in valleys, but they generally looked very much alike.

We had not passed anyone or anything coming the other way along our series of ledges, and I asked the chief of our expedition, the eighty-year-old Sarkal, why that was. 'Plenty of other ways,' he said 'none easier, none more difficult. Nobody goes by a straight road. If you look, you will see that these ledges are everywhere. A man could pass his brother twenty times a day, and never choose the same ledge.'

We were stopping more and more frequently for rests and a smoke, once we got used to the most unpleasant sensation that I called mountain sickness (for want of a better word) and Sarkal called *Devghar* – mountain demon. If this had been a test of endurance, I could never have made it, because I could not have kept up with mountaineers who were used to maintaining a good pace, such as the Kafirs whom I was later to see. But our expedition was no heroic one, and the spirit of getting somewhere fast would have been completely alien to them. I was glad that Sarkal agreed with my Arab proverb *al ajala min ashshaitaan,* 'hastening is sent by the Devil'.

Three solid days of mountains, with never a valley through which we could pass. Wild and very cold streams to bathe in; dried fruit and nuts most of the time, no contact with any other human being, although we were passing through a populated area. 'This had better be worth it,' or words to that effect, were what I had been repeating to myself. When the idea was firmly in my head and I was thinking of little else, I said to Katticha, the half-Kafir lad who was with us as general assistant to Sarkal: 'Is it worth it?'

'Worth is within you.' He was a philosopher at the age of sixteen.

But I could hardly ask for my money back. I still had most of what I had handed the 'banker' in Pakistan, which had been duly paid out by a Sufi *khazanchi* (treasurer) of the Ishan's community. Then we began to see people: Kafiristanis at that. The first one was a tall, slightly bent figure carrying a huge basket on his back, walking down the 'road' with a faraway look in his eyes, and humming a very Western kind of air. *'Saam'*, he said, which I took to be the local variation of 'Salam alaikum' or Peace upon you.

'Butter' said Sarkal, over his shoulder as the man passed us stretched flat against the cliff-face to let him by. 'They collect butter, pack it in baskets and take it to market. Same with walnuts, fruit and nuts and a lot of other things. They do not eat fish, because according to their ancient beliefs they are unclean.'

I had had a good look at my first Kafiristani as he passed. He was fair-skinned with grey or blue eyes, very Western-looking indeed.

'Looks like a farangi,' I said to Sarkal, forgetting that I was a 'Frank' myself. 'Yes, many of them do. People say that they are descended from the people of Alexander, but I don't know. They sit on chairs, like the Franks, though.'

At last we seemed to be descending steadily, and the air was less full of cold, and that is the only way to put it, because the experience was a new one to me. We were just going through a most picturesque rift between two standing rocks, which looked as if they had been specially split to make way for the trail when I glimpsed a shower of blossoms, a strip of green, a clump of trees, a fairyland, a garden growing wild, a valley so delicious that I could hardly believe that it was real. I gasped at the sight.

We were really in inaccessible Nuristan now, in the valley known locally as Margal. The Nuristanis, I found, had no name for their country as a whole, but referred to various parts of it by names, some of which were not generally accepted. Margal, for instance, was called this by its inhabitants, who comprised six or seven villages. The people to the East called it Chantai, and those to the West, Innia. I did not ask what the inhabitants of the north and south called it. This, according to Sarkal, would not help greatly, because Chatai meant simply 'smaller', and he thought that even Margal meant something like 'changing'. The implications of what was smaller than what, and when and why a place changed, were altogether too much for me, although they did disabuse my mind of the first assumption that a place with so many names might point to an unusually rich language.

The largest village was to be our headquarters, and I was taken to see the headman. His house was stone-built, and he seemed to be of an Aryan type of extraction. This middle-aged man with full whiskers and twinkling eyes spoke a good deal of Persian and Pushtu, and was known as Dauud (David) or, sometimes, it seemed, Dauun. He wore deerskin boots, which looked something like Redskin ones, a cap woven from soft wool and shaped like a bucket, which rolled up and sat back on his head. His clothes were a shirt with two cloaks on top, one cotton, the upper one wool. He and his family drank wine, which the Kafirs have always drunk, sacrificed to Gysh, the wine-god, of whom they had a wooden effigy. This was of very rough workmanship, but the chief said that this did not matter, so long as it had a crown. More important than Gysh was Immra, much more powerful than Gysh, who had no proper representation, because he lived in the clouds and nobody really knew his shape. How, as he asked me, could one make a model of something when it had never been seen? This seemed a logical approach. But had Gysh ever been seen?

Certainly, Gysh had been seen. He was often seen. He worked miracles and gave victory in war. He would appear sometimes when one least expected it, but not infrequently in the old days when wine-feasts were given in his honour.

The village was undistinguished, though flourishing. In the market place wheat, lentils, maize and beans were sold, as well as many kinds of dried fruits, especially apricots. The butter, which we had carried by a Kafir some days ago, was excellent. The houses were simple, and not as 'European' as one would have thought from the assertion that the Kafirs had tables and chairs. They sat on benches and also ate with sticks, and this did give some sort of impression of a Western meal, but only just. I had an opportunity of talking to a great many Kafirs who understand Persian. Their own language seemed at times to sound a little like Hindi, but the effect of Persian and Pushtu was being felt, and they often used a word from one of these languages when at a loss for a phrase.

The money used is Afghan currency, and people prefer coins to the notes (often of very small denomination) which are current in most parts of Afghanistan.

The whole atmosphere of the valley, and of other valleys which I was able to see, was strikingly reminiscent of what one might have thought that 'Merrie England' looked like. In the first place most of the trees and plants which are familiar in Britain grow here. The dress of the people is not so much Oriental as what one would consider a 'peasant' anywhere to be dressed in. The women wear blouses and full skirts; the men trousers and leather belts. On market day, people revolve around a gaily-coloured and decorated post which, by a very small effort of imagination, becomes a maypole. Performing bears, men with bows (longbows) and arrows, people selling cups of strong liquor dyed purple with some plant, all contribute towards a general effect which is at once bizarre and almost familiar. The nearest I could get to this feeling was to imagine that someone had described in words to someone else what the Middle Ages were like, and he had in turn made all the costumes and decor for some sort of pageant or simple theatrical show.

The Sufis' settlement was half a mile away from the chief's house, a large, stone-built building erected around an open space. We made our way there after eating a token meal of curds with the headman. Here the *Murshid* (Guide) a tall, spare man from the Kabul area, who had lived in Nuristan, he told me, for nearly thirty years. That must have meant that he came here almost as a child. He spoke a number of languages, including two which were spoken by the Kafirs. When he went out, he wore over his shirt instead of the usual robe a blue military-type tunic with epaulettes, which for some reason established or maintained his temporal (if not spiritual) position with the surrounding citizenry.

I found the Murshid unusually willing to answer questions on all matters of Sufi thought and practise, as well as on the Kafirs, about all of which he clearly knew a great deal. The story of Sufi settlement in Nuristan was that shortly before the Afghan conquest of the country a number of missions of Sufis from the Western Hindu Kush area had been sent to contact remnants of mystical groups whom they believed to be centred there. In the event, and after terrible opposition – because the Kafirs instinctively killed any Moslem whom they saw – three small groups of anchorites were found. They were Christians, and seemed to have had no contact with the outside world since the Islamic conquest of Eastern Persia in the seventh century. Communication with them was difficult, because there was no common language. The problem was solved by the initiative of the Christian monks, who discovered common words, or words of common origin, in their form of Persian and that spoken by the Sufis.

The great-great uncle of our host was one of the mission, and he had stayed in Kafiristan for twenty years, until he died. He was by then fluent both in the local tongues and that of the Christian community. Their story was quite interesting. They fled from the area of Bactria (modern Balkh), thinking that the Antichrist had come when they heard of the approach of the Arab armies First they went to Kabul, which had held out for some time. Later they escaped, and were befriended by a party of Kafir refugees who had settled near Kabul but were now forced back into the mountains. They learned the language of the Kafirs among whom they lived, and split up into three bodies, each under a teacher. These self-perpetuating communities had converted to Christianity, no doubt for some reason of their own beliefs, only enough Kafirs to replace those who died. In order to maintain their religion and their customs, each convert was taught the armchair Persian language which the original refugees spoke. This explained how the community had survived into the eighteen-nineties – over eleven hundred years – in considerable isolation.

The knowledge of their existence had seeped into Afghanistan proper through the conversion of peripheral Kafirs to Islam, people who generally settled in Afghanistan when they forsook the faith of their fathers. One such man, who had joined the Azamiia community of Sufis, told what he could of the recluses from the ancient times to the Sufi sheikh of the time. The result was the Sufi mission, which must have taken place about 1880 or perhaps a little later.

These Christians eventually joined the Sufis, whom they considered to have very similar practices to their own. According to the Murshid, these 'old Christians' maintained rituals very like Sufi ones, but very different from those of present-day Christianity. Whether this part of the tale was accurate, one has no means of knowing. There is little doubt that there were many sects of early Christianity which differed in very important respects from those which we know today. One characteristic of the Christian survival was, according to the Sufi chief, that sacramental wine was drunk in large quantities, after being dedicated by the worshipers, and was thought to produce a state of spiritual exaltation. When I reminded him that this habit could have been 'contamination' from Kafir religion, where something similar was practised, he at once agreed.

The majority of the Sufis of Kafiristan were local people, from both sections of the population : the free and the (formerly) slave. They spent comparatively little time in the 'monastery', only visiting it for a part of their 'development' and then returning to their various worldly tasks. There was no special difference between the ideas and routines of the Western Hindu Kush Sufis and those settled in Kafiristan : which was to be expected if the settlement were of such comparatively late age. The members were not at all worried about the probability that, as the country developed, life would change very much for the inhabitants of Kafiristan. The general attitude was that life had to change, and people had to change. If the practice could not change to keep pace with the tempo or rhythm of life, or if it were not actually ahead of that tempo, the practice must die out; and should die out.

It was here that I first felt in a sense of certainty that a practice which grew with the practitioners, or which seemed to harmonise with what the rest of the world was doing, must continue to have an influence upon the world. I was, in other words, being influenced by the sense of unity and certainty which characterised this branch (or should it be root?) of the Sufi Way.

I had become more acclimatised every day to the rarefied atmosphere, and little by little the sheer breathtaking beauty of Nuristan grew upon me. The contrast between the still snow-

covered peaks of the mountains and the lower slopes with thickly
growing deodar and pine trees, then the soft, lush, almost Irish
grass caught my heart each time I ran my eyes across this rich-
ness.

I formed the habit of taking long walks, especially after I was
told that, with the retreating snow, the white leopards were less
to be seen in the valleys. It was on one of these expeditions,
when I was thinking of nothing much apart from the primroses
which continued to appear into that highland Summer, that I
first saw the Qizil-Baba.

He was a good deal taller than the six-foot attributed to him;
red-bearded (Qizil-Baba means 'red father') and dressed in a
long white woollen cloak with patches sewn inside it. Throughout my journeys in this country I had, from time to time, heard
people say, 'The Qizil-Baba lives in Nuristan'; or 'As says the
Qizil-Baba, he of Kafiristan'. But, when I had asked further
about him, the answer was always evasive. I had long ago decided that he was some sort of legendary, or even literary, figure.

He came striding down a small wooded valley, from the direction of a turreted building set against a rock, like three corners
of a fortress pressed against the mountain-wall. Which was, as
I later saw, exactly what it was. There was a huge cave where
the mountain-ledge broke against the turf. Across and in front of
this the three-sided fort had been built, of grey stone.

I raised my hand in salutation, and he changed direction,
turning towards me a look of gravity and interest. As he was
within five feet of me I realised that he was over sixty years old.
On the little finger of his upraised right hand I saw a small gold
signet-ring. This was most unusual; partly because Moslems
hardly ever wear gold rings, partly because it was not an
Oriental ring. He spoke to me in barbarous Pushtu, with an
intonation that surely had nothing to do with Afghanistan or
the Pathans.

As he was saying, looking at my clothes, 'Mullah Saheb, may
you never be tired!', I suddenly recognised the accent. The
Qizil-Baba was a Scotsman!

'I know about you,' he said in the soft and cultivated accents
of the scholar, 'and I would like to talk to you before I die.'

He was leading me with a firm step, for all the world like a
don taking a stroll with an under-graduate across the quad, in

the direction of his fort. I said that I hoped that the day of his death might be far off. 'Far nearer than you think,' he said, 'even if only because I am in my late eighties.' He looked so strong and sprightly for that age that I could hardly bring myself to believe him. But I said no more until we were inside the house.

It was a house, too, for all its forbidding outside. Piece by piece, all with his own hands, the Baba had, as he explained to me, panelled the entire area of the inner cave. It now looked something like the baronial hall of a Scottish castle. There were even glass-paned windows, something I saw nowhere else in Nuristan. The outer wall itself was doubled, and constituted a series of three fairly large rooms. One contained books, neatly labelled and arranged on shelves: books in English, other Western languages, Persian and Arabic – and a few in Indian languages. The middle room was whitewashed, with nothing in it beyond a large white fleece in the centre of the floor 'Ma meditation-room', and the third chamber was a simple kitchen-cum-workroom. As to the function or use of the cave itself I could make no guess.

His name, he told me, was David Alexander MacNeill ('and verra strange it was of ma parents te allow such initials to burrden a man'). His story was briefly told, though it probably had a far greater content of excitement than he would give it.

The Qizil-Baba was already in his forties when the First World War broke out. Giving up his job with a firm of solicitors in Glasgow, he volunteered and saw much action in France. He was badly wounded and invalided out of the Army in 1917, when he first met an Indian who was preaching a form of Sufism. He studied with him for three or four years. After the War he followed him to France, where the mystic had decided to stay. The Sufi system followed by this teacher seemed to MacNeill to lack something. It did not accord with what was written about Sufism in the available books on the subject. Worse still, it was largely based upon collecting people together on what MacNeill thought to be the 'lowest common factor'; the mutual belief in religion. MacNeill was in a dilemma. He realised that music, given by these Sufis as a means of entry into higher insights, was something that Sufi literature regarded as an incidental. 'And I also knew that, whatever the intentions of these gentlemen, they were attracting idolators of themselves.' But he also thought that there was something very profound, perhaps 'of surpassing importance to humanity', in Sufism.

'So I regard my first Indian teachers as people perhaps destined to stimulate real interest in real Sufism, by their very manner of preaching a Way which was not Sufism' he said to me, turning his expressive eyes to look squarely into mine.

MacNeill betook himself to India, to seek the sources of the Sufi teaching. By this time, no longer a really young man, he had little means of livelihood and earned less respect either from the British residents or from the native population. He took a job looking after the basic education of the children of an Indian maharaja.

I had set out to visit Mecca; and this, instead of being an end, had proved to be a beginning. Then I thought that I would collect material, because there was so very little in print anywhere, about what the Sufis were doing and thinking today. When this was done, there remained the conviction that here, beyond the superficial outwardness of the cult, there was something active in the human mind which might, for all I knew, outlast many another, more ephemeral one.

Did this mean that a hidden tradition, while it was practised, was true because it had the vitality to continue in spite of change in the world? This I did not know; and did not much care, because experience of Sufi communities, exercises and ways had shown me that if anything was true at all, it was what the Sufis had unceasingly dinned into my ears: that you cannot judge everything merely because you think that you are qualified – and perhaps even less if someone else tells you that you are qualified to do so.

I made the trek back to the comparative civilisation of Pakistan without enthusiasm for any more excursions into a world which belonged to itself. The Sufi is right when, talking about other Sufis, he says: 'I have my Way, which suffices me, in accordance with my place in the world, and the part of the world where I find myself.'

FURTHER READING

Arberry, Professor A. J., *Discourses of Rumi,* New York (Samuel Weiser). Translations of some address by Rumi, from Persian, by the well-known Professor of Arabic at Cambridge. Valuable source of material on Rumi, but contains mistakes. Academic production.

Bennett, J. G., *A Spiritual Psychology,* London (Hodder & Stoughton), 1964. Primarily dealing with the 'Subud' phenomenon, this is a mathematician's attempt to relate the teachings of Sufism, Gurdjieff and Subud, although emanating from Indonesia, is based upon a Sufi model, and is evidently a deteriorated form. In this and other books, Mr. Bennett seems to have grasped that there is a connection between these philosophies, but does not go so far as to say that Sufism is the origin of them all.

Burckhardt, T., *An Introduction to Sufi Doctrine,* translated by D. M. Matheson, Lahore (Ashraf) 1959. Claiming to introduce the reader to the doctrines of Sufism, this small book is in reality a survey of the application of Sufi ideas in an entirely Mohammedan milieu. References are made to Christianity and various esoteric teachings. Interesting but the bias is towards synthesis on a lower level of spirituality.

Collin Smith, R., *Sol Booklets,* Mexico, 1954. A series of five booklets in English, in which the Author deals with the connexion between Christianity, the Whirling Dervishes, the Alchemists and other teachings. Although his information about the linking of these traditions must have come from an informed source, the texts themselves show that they are only an attempt at making sense of the common denominators. The Author tries to use the Sufi nine-angled figure in these illustrated booklets.

Gurdjieff, G., *All and Everything,* New York (E. P. Dutton & Co.), 1964. Elaborate and wordy (1238 pages) means of wrapping up a number of Sufi and Dervish exercises and technical terms.

Hammerskjold, Dag, *Markings,* translated by L. Sjoberg and

Further Reading

W. H. Auden, New York (Alfred A. Knopf), 1964. The late Secretary-General of the United Nations writes on matters connecting with Sufi ideas (such as 'action necessary for mystics today'). Quotes Rumi.

Holmboe, Knud, *Desert Encounter,* translated by Helga Holbek, London (Harrap), 1936. The author, a Danish Anthropologist, describes conversations with Sufis in North Africa, among much other material. The author is a Moslem convert, and the bias is towards Islam.

Manyasigh, M., *Nasreddin Hoca,* Istanbul (Maarif Basimevi), not dated. Some stories of Nasreddin, perhaps the first public print in which the role of this Dervish figure as a cloak for esoteric teaching is hinted at.

Massignon, Professor Louis, *Le Diwan D'al-Hallaj,* Paris (Paul Geuthner), 1955. Much interesting material, including a passage in which Hallaj, the greatest Sufi martyr, shows that his beliefs are essentially identical with Christianity.

Nicoll, Dr. Maurice, *Psychological Commentaries,* 3 vols., New York (Samuel Weiser), 1957. Sufi teachings, largely collected from Ouspensky and Gurdjieff, arranged as lectures. The material uses ideas from the Sufi Attar and other teachers, but the method of presentation ignores Sufic practice, and is therefore 'amateur' work.

Nott, C. S., *The Conference of the Birds,* London (Routledge & Kegan Paul), 1954 and 1961. English translation of a French translation of one version of Attar's Sufi classic. This rendering does not preserve the psychological meaning, but makes good reading taken as a religious poem. Some terms in the Glossary are inaccurate.

Ouspensky, P. D., *The Psychology of Man's Possible Evolution,* New York (Alfred A. Knopf), 1974. The Russian philosopher quotes Sufi teachings and uses some Sufic methods of argument in these collected lectures to refer to religious and psychological systems. Slightly arid, because the treatment is intellectual. Not a source-book.

Rice, Cyprian, O. P., *The Persian Sufis,* New York (Humanities Press), 1964. Short survey from the Catholic point of view. The Author is a Dominican, and the book has the Imprimatur of the Dominican and Diocesan authorities in Rome. Not based on personal experience.

Robinson, J. A. (Bishop of Woolwich), *Honest to God,* Philadelphia (Westminster Press), 1963. The Bishop follows Sufic methods of thought first used by Al-Ghazzali (d.1111 A.D.) applying them to Christian problems in a philosophical manner.

Stace, W. T., *The Teachings of the Mystics,* New York (Mentor Books), 1960. Literary selections from mystical writings. Fair number of extracts from Sufi classics, but very brief. Secondary material.

Teilhard de Chardin. Father Pierre, *The Phenomenon of Man,* New York (Harper & Row), 1965. A modern Western thinker's attempt to develop the theory of psychological evolution put forth by the Sufis. Not, therefore, original, but most interesting.

Vett, Carl, *Dervish Diary,* translated by E. W. Hathaway, Los Angeles (K. K. Mogensen), 1953. Personal account of time spent with the more religious type of Nakshibendi Sufis in Turkey. The bias is towards occultism.

Walker, Kenneth, *Diagnosis of Man,* London (Penguin Books), 1962. A psychological work by a surgeon, using Sufi references, such as the 'Elephant in the Dark' story of Rumi's. Influenced by the Russian philosopher P. D. Ouspensky.